DEMOCRACY AND
THE GOSPEL OF WEALTH

Problems in American Civilization

PREPARED UNDER THE EDITORSHIP OF

Earl Latham
George Rogers Taylor
George F. Whicher

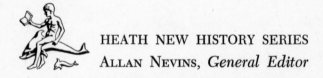

HEATH NEW HISTORY SERIES
ALLAN NEVINS, *General Editor*

Democracy and the Gospel of Wealth

EDITED WITH AN INTRODUCTION BY

Gail Kennedy

Problems in American Civilization

READINGS SELECTED BY THE
DEPARTMENT OF AMERICAN STUDIES
AMHERST COLLEGE

D. C. HEATH AND COMPANY: Boston

Offices

Boston   New York   Chicago   Dallas

Atlanta   San Francisco   London

INTRODUCTION

WALT WHITMAN proclaimed in his first preface to *Leaves of Grass* (1855):

The Americans of all nations at any time upon the earth have probably the fullest poetical nature. The United States themselves are essentially the greatest poem.

And a little farther on he added:

Other states indicate themselves in their deputies . . . but the genius of the United States is not best or most in its executives or legislatures, nor in its ambassadors or authors or colleges or churches or parlors, nor even in its newspapers or inventors . . . but always most in the common people. . . . The pride of the United States leaves the wealth and finesse of the cities and all the returns of commerce and agriculture and all the magnitude of geography or shows of exterior victory to enjoy the breed of full-sized men or one full-sized man unconquerable and simple.

Three decades later, Andrew Carnegie in the opening paragraph of his *Triumphant Democracy* (1886) made another proclamation:

The old nations of the earth creep on at a snail's pace; the Republic thunders past with the rush of the express. The United States, the growth of a single century, has already reached the foremost rank among nations, and is destined soon to out-distance all others in the race. In population, in wealth, in annual savings, and in public credit; in freedom from debt, in agriculture, and in manufactures, America already leads the civilized world.

What had happened? Was this boasted prosperity the outcome of that Civil War which Whitman believed was the final proof and triumph of *his* democracy? Was this industrial progress the vision of America that had inspired Jefferson, Jackson, and Lincoln? Walt Whitman, looking upon the orgy of acquisitive exploitation that followed the Civil War, saw material success producing a spiritual corruption that threatened to destroy our democracy. To his penetrating gaze the society of the Gilded Age appeared "cankered, crude, superstitious, and rotten. Political or law-made society is, and private, or voluntary society is also. In any vigor, the element of the moral conscience, the most important, the verteber to State or man, seems to me either entirely lacking, or seriously enfeebled or ingrown." A haunting doubt began to possess him: "Then comes the terrible query, and will not be denied, Is not Democracy of human rights humbug after all — Are these flippant people with hearts of rags and souls of chalk, are these worth preaching for and dying for upon the cross?" It was to still this doubt, to come to grips with the worst that any cynic could assert about the greedy materialism of postwar America, that Whitman wrote his *Democratic Vistas* (1871).

It was a painfully hard book for him to write. The easy exuberance of the earlier Whitman is gone. The future seems dark and uncertain. One thing is clear. Unless the "hoggish, cheating, bedbug qualities" of the age can be overcome by a revival of the democratic idealism that carried us through the Civil War, this experiment in which the future of humanity is on trial will fail.

Carnegie, on the contrary, had no such doubts. He viewed this same material success as a *means* to social progress. Thereby the standard of living for all is raised. It is true, he admits, that the price we pay for modern industrialism is great; yet men of great wealth are not "robber barons," harbingers of a new feudalism, but trustees whose duty it is to devote their talents to the common good. This, in his opinion, is "the true Gospel concerning Wealth, obedience to which is destined some day to solve the problem of the Rich and the Poor, and to bring 'Peace on earth, among men Good-Will.' "

While it was the struggle between the "few" and the "many" that underlay the party battles of the era of Jefferson and the age of Jackson, few seriously believed at that time that democracy itself was endangered. But the Civil War was in truth a "second American Revolution," an economic revolution which many have felt has increasingly jeopardized our freedoms. Hence, our political history since the Civil War is marked by a succession of attempts to control the great corporate enterprises that gradually came to dominate our economy, — beginning with the Granger movement in the seventies, continuing with the Green Back Party and the Populist Party of the eighties and early nineties, and resulting in the capture of the Democratic Party under the leadership of Bryan, the infil-

tration of the Republican Party in the form of Theodore Roosevelt's "Square Deal," and going on from there, to the "New Freedom" of Wilson, Franklin D. Roosevelt's "New Deal," and the "Fair Deal" of Harry S. Truman.

Both Whitman and Carnegie were attempting in their wholly different ways to deal with the same basic problem, the fate of a democracy that historically was based on substantial *equality*, a predominantly rural nation of farmers, mechanics, shopkeepers, and small manufacturers, as it was in process of becoming an urban and industrial society increasingly dominated by the "captains of industry" who control great corporations.

This is a situation which, obviously, generates many cross-currents of opinion. The remainder of the readings here included are chosen to illustrate various interpretations of the issue as it is presented by the contrast between Whitman and Carnegie. These readings fall into three groups: (1) selections from two contemporary historians which provide a critical survey of the thought and culture of the period; (2) a group of writings which defend the gospel of wealth; (3) some typical criticisms of that gospel. Both the proponents and the critics of the gospel of wealth base their cases upon one or more of three lines of argument which they respectively defend or attack. These are: (1) the religious argument — the Pauline doctrine of stewardship; (2) the economic argument — the efficiency of laissez faire; (3) the argument from "evolution" — the survival of the fittest.

The selections in the first group are from Vernon L. Parrington's *Main Currents in American Thought* and Ralph Henry Gabriel's *The Course of American Democratic Thought*. The first selection from Parrington, "The American Scene," is the introductory portion of his third volume, *The Beginnings of Critical Realism in America*. In these pages he graphically describes the Gilded Age. In the next selection, his chapter entitled "The Afterglow of the Enlightenment — Walt Whitman," he discusses Whitman's efforts to maintain the idealism of Jefferson and Emerson in an age of business enterprise. The last selection in this group is Gabriel's brilliant chapter on "The Gospel of Wealth of the Gilded Age."

The second group of readings begins with an article entitled "The Relation of Wealth to Morals" (1901) by the Right Reverend William Lawrence, Episcopal Bishop of Massachusetts. This article is an example of the defense of Carnegie's thesis in terms of the Pauline doctrine of the stewardship of wealth. It is God's will, the Bishop argues, that some men should attain great wealth; and, "in the long run, it is only to the man of morality that wealth comes." Such men are the chosen reapers in the vineyard of the Lord. Hence Bishop Lawrence is able to conclude: "Material prosperity is helping to make the national character sweeter, more joyous, more unselfish, more Christlike."

Next, we have an example of the defense of laissez-faire capitalism on the grounds of economic theory. John Bates Clark, one of the leading economists of this period, had argued in his book, *The Philosophy of Wealth* (1886), that *if* (and the "if" is all-important) an open market and free competition are maintained, the result will be a just distribution of the goods that society produces and a steady rise in the standard of living for everyone who contributes to their production. The rich will grow richer, but so will the poor. In the selection reprinted below, a popular article entitled

"The Society of the Future" (1901), Clark carried his optimism to such lengths as to conjecture that within fifty years the working man might be able to go to the mountains on a day's wages or on those of a hundred days take a European tour.

William Graham Sumner's essay, "The Concentration of Wealth: Its Economic Justification" (1902), appears next in the readings. Sumner, professor of political and social science at Yale, was the leading American disciple of Herbert Spencer and one of the founders of the new science of sociology. His defense of laissez-faire capitalism is based on the hypothesis that "the social order is fixed by laws of nature precisely analogous to those of the physical order. The most that man can do is by his ignorance and conceit to mar the operation of the social laws." With his cultural determinism Sumner combines a Spencerian theory of "evolution." From this base he arrives at virtually the same practical conclusions regarding the beneficence of capitalism as those of the theological school.

The final reading in this second group, Elbert Hubbard's *A Message to Garcia* (1899), is included as the most conspicuous example of the "success literature" that had such tremendous vogue during this period, — a time when all boys read the Alger books and dreamed of emulating their young heroes. Huge editions of Hubbard's little tract were printed for mass distribution by business firms. Perhaps as many as forty million copies, in all, were issued.

The first selection in the final group of readings is by Charles S. Peirce, one of the seminal minds in American philosophy, originator of the "pragmatism" that was later to be brilliantly developed by William James and John Dewey. In this excerpt from one of his essays,

"Evolutionary Love" (1903), he contradicts the assertion of Bishop Lawrence that "Godliness is in league with riches" and sharply opposes the Christian law of love to Spencer's theory of evolution, that competition produces a "survival of the fittest."

Next appears W. J. Ghent's article, "The Next Step: A Benevolent Feudalism" (1902). From this article he developed his book, *Our Benevolent Feudalism*, published in the same year. Ghent works out the parallel between the new industrial order and the hierarchical society of the Middle Ages with great ingenuity. By putting a description of things as they then were in the form of a *prediction*, he shows, with an irony comparable to Veblen's in *The Theory of the Leisure Class*, that the real outcome of the doctrine of the stewardship of wealth is a "benevolent" feudalism.

Thorstein Veblen is the archenemy of the gospel of wealth. He might well be said to have dedicated himself to the "higher criticism" of that doctrine. All of his writings are variations on this theme. The selection included here, "The Captain of Industry," is from *Absentee Ownership and Business Enterprise in Recent Times* (1923), but two of his most important books, books in which his point of view is fully developed, *The Theory of the Leisure Class* (1899) and *The Theory of Business Enterprise* (1904), appeared at the turn of the century. A pupil of John Bates Clark, he produced in his early essay, "The Limitations of Marginal Utility," a drastic analysis of Clark's economic theory. *The Theory of the Leisure Class* is an attempt far more profound than Ghent's to expose the feudal character of a regime of private ownership and pecuniary emulation. Veblen's chapter on "The Captain of Industry" is based on the same concep-

tion of "the laws of societal evolution" from which Sumner deduced that the captain of industry was a *necessary* consequence of the development of industry. Veblen argues that he was also a *transient* consequence. The evolutionary process has supplanted him by forcing a division of his functions. The old-fashioned "captain of industry" has been replaced by the modern "businessman." And between industry and business there is an antagonism that, in Veblen's view, totally contradicts the doctrine of the stewardship of wealth.

The last word has been left to that incomparable observer of the American scene, Mr. Dooley. The Catholic Irishman as he leans over the bar in his darkened cool saloon on Archey Road takes but a dim view of the Scotch evangelist of wealth. Mr. Dooley's final verdict on "Andhrew Carnaygie" is that "Ivry time he gives a libry he gives himsilf away in a speech."

This problem has been presented through writings of the period between the Civil War and the turn of the century. Some of the terms of that controversy may seem remote to us, but there can be no doubt about the contemporary relevance of the main issue. These writers all agree on one fundamental point, that private enterprise is invested with a public interest, that somehow or other those who control our industries must fulfill their responsibilities to the community. On March 3, 1947, the *New York Times* printed under the headline "Future of Free Enterprise in World Found Uncertain" a group of reports from its correspondents. All but one of the nineteen nations included in this survey had established complete government control of industry or were moving towards a greater degree of such control. Only in Canada could private enterprise be said to function with anything like the freedom that obtains in the United States.

Historically our democratic liberties were won in conjunction with economic liberties. It is a real question whether the freedom of the market is not an essential condition of such precious rights as freedom of speech. Caught in a rising tide of collectivism, whether it be the privately controlled collectivism of Big Business or the publicly administered collectivism of the Corporate State, the issue becomes each decade more dangerously insistent: can our industrial system be subordinated to the purposes of a democratic social order? Many people still believe with Carnegie that private business can be trusted to operate, on the whole, in a way that will truly serve the public interest, that the men who control our great corporations recognize their responsibility for the common welfare. Others will argue, with Carnegie's opponents, that this is a moral responsibility too great for private citizens to bear, that the state must intervene to insure that the public interest will be observed. How, as between these alternatives, the *individual* will fare, what choice will best preserve those rights and freedoms that such men as Jefferson, Emerson, and Whitman stood for, is a question each one of us must try to answer.

[NOTE: The statement by Arthur M. Schlesinger, Jr., on p. xii is quoted from *The Age of Jackson* (Boston, 1945), p. 505, by permission of Little, Brown and Company.]

CONTENTS

THE CLASH OF ISSUES

Andrew Carnegie states his optimistic creed of
philanthropic business enterprise:

"Thus is the problem of Rich and Poor to be solved. The laws of accumulation will be left free; the laws of distribution free. Individualism will continue, but the millionaire will be but a trustee for the poor; intrusted for a season with a great part of the increased wealth of the community, but administering it for the community far better than it could or would have done for itself."

A bishop concurs:

"In the long run, it is only to the man of morality that wealth comes. . . . Godliness is in league with riches."

— THE RIGHT REVEREND WILLIAM LAWRENCE

And a railroad president declared during the
coal strike of 1902:

"The rights and interests of the laboring man will be protected and cared for, not by the labor agitators, but by the Christian men to whom God in His infinite wisdom, has given control of the property interests of the country."

— GEORGE F. BAER

But a philosopher disagrees:

"Here, then, is the issue. The gospel of Christ says that progress comes from every individual merging his individuality in sympathy with his neighbors. On the other side, the conviction of the nineteenth century is that progress takes place by virtue of every individual's striving for himself with all his might and trampling his neighbor under foot whenever he gets a chance to do so. This may accurately be called the Gospel of Greed."

— CHARLES S. PEIRCE

And a historian attempts to clarify the issue:

"American democracy has come to accept the struggle among competing groups for the control of the state as a positive virtue — indeed, as the only foundation for liberty. The business community has been ordinarily the most powerful of these groups, and liberalism in America has been ordinarily the movement on the part of the other sections of society to restrain the power of the business community. This was the tradition of Jefferson and Jackson, and it has been the basic meaning of American liberalism."

— ARTHUR M. SCHLESINGER, JR.

Andrew Carnegie: WEALTH

THE problem of our age is the proper administration of wealth, so that the ties of brotherhood may still bind together the rich and poor in harmonious relationship. The conditions of human life have not only been changed, but revolutionized, within the past few hundred years. In former days there was little difference between the dwelling, dress, food, and environment of the chief and those of his retainers. The Indians are to-day where civilized man then was. When visiting the Sioux, I was led to the wigwam of the chief. It was just like the others in external appearance, and even within the difference was trifling between it and those of the poorest of his braves. The contrast between the palace of the millionaire and the cottage of the laborer with us to-day measures the change which has come with civilization.

This change, however, is not to be deplored, but welcomed as highly beneficial. It is well, nay, essential for the progress of the race, that the houses of some should be homes for all that is highest and best in literature and the arts, and for all the refinements of civilization, rather than that none should be so. Much better this great irregularity than universal squalor. Without wealth there can be no Maecenas. The "good old times" were not good old times. Neither master nor servant was as well situated then as to-day. A relapse to old conditions would be disastrous to both — not the least so to him who serves — and would sweep away civilization with it. But whether the change be for good or ill, it is upon us, beyond our power to alter, and therefore to be accepted and made the best of. It is a waste of time to criticise the inevitable.

It is easy to see how the change has come. One illustration will serve for almost every phase of the cause. In the manufacture of products we have the whole story. It applies to all combinations of human industry, as stimulated and enlarged by the inventions of this scientific age. Formerly articles were manufactured at the domestic hearth or in small shops which formed part of the household. The master and his apprentices worked side by side, the latter living with the master, and therefore subject to the same conditions. When these apprentices rose to be masters, there was little or no change in their mode of life, and they, in turn, educated in the same routine succeeding apprentices. There was, substantially, social equality, and even political equality, for those engaged in industrial pursuits had then little or no political voice in the State.

But the inevitable result of such a mode of manufacture was crude articles at high prices. To-day the world obtains commodities of excellent quality at prices which even the generation preceding this would have deemed incredible. In the commercial world similar causes have produced similar results, and the race is benefited thereby. The poor enjoy what the rich could not before afford. What were the luxuries have become the necessaries of life. The laborer has now more comforts than the farmer had a few generations ago. The farmer has more luxuries than the landlord had, and is more richly clad and better housed. The landlord has books and pictures rarer, and appointments more artistic, than the King could then obtain.

The price we pay for this salutary change is, no doubt, great. We assemble thousands of operatives in the factory, in the mine, and in the counting-house, of whom the employer can know little or nothing, and to whom the employer is little better than a myth. All intercourse between them is at an end. Rigid Castes are formed, and, as usual, mutual ignorance breeds mutual distrust. Each Caste is without sympathy for the other, and ready to credit anything disparaging in regard to it. Under the law of competition, the employer of thousands is forced into the strictest economies, among which the rates paid to labor figure prominently, and often there is friction between the employer and the employed, between capital and labor, between rich and poor. Human society loses homogeneity.

The price which society pays for the law of competition, like the price it pays for cheap comforts and luxuries, is also great; but the advantages of this law are also greater still, for it is to this law that we owe our wonderful material development, which brings improved conditions in its train. But, whether the law be benign or not, we must say of it, as we say of the change in the conditions of men to which we have referred: It is here; we cannot evade it; no substitutes for it have been found; and while the law may be sometimes hard for the individual, it is best for the race, because it insures the survival of the fittest in every

department. We accept and welcome, therefore, as conditions to which we must accommodate ourselves, great inequality of environment, the concentration of business, industrial and commercial, in the hands of a few, and the law of competition between these, as being not only beneficial, but essential for the future progress of the race. Having accepted these, it follows that there must be great scope for the exercise of special ability in the merchant and in the manufacturer who has to conduct affairs upon a great scale. That this talent for organization and management is rare among men, is proved by the fact that it invariably secures for its possessor enormous rewards, no matter where or under what laws or conditions. The experienced in affairs always rate the MAN whose services can be obtained as a partner as not only the first consideration, but such as to render the question of his capital scarcely worth considering, for such men soon create capital; while, without the special talent required, capital soon takes wings. Such men become interested in firms or corporations using millions; and estimating only simple interest to be made upon the capital invested, it is inevitable that their income must exceed their expenditures, and that they must accumulate wealth. Nor is there any middle ground which such men can occupy, because the great manufacturing or commercial concern which does not earn at least interest upon its capital soon becomes bankrupt. It must either go forward or fall behind: to stand still is impossible. It is a condition essential for its successful operation that it should be thus far profitable, and even that, in addition to interest on capital, it should make profit. It is a law, as certain as any of the others named, that men possessed of this peculiar talent for affairs, under the free play of economic forces, must, of necessity, soon be in receipt of more revenue than can be judiciously expended upon themselves; and this law is as beneficial for the race as the others.

Objections to the foundations upon which society is based are not in order, because the condition of the race is better with these than it has been with any others which have been tried. Of the effect of any new substitutes proposed we cannot be sure. The Socialist or Anarchist who seeks to overturn present conditions is to be regarded as attacking the foundation upon which civilization itself rests, for civilization took its start from the day that the capable, industrious workman said to his incompetent and lazy fellow, "If thou dost not sow, thou shalt not reap," and thus ended primitive Communism by separating the drones from the bees. One who studies this subject will soon be brought face to face with the conclusion that upon the sacredness of property civilization itself depends — the right of the laborer to his hundred dollars in the savings bank, and equally the legal right of the millionaire to his millions. To those who propose to substitute Communism for this intense Individualism the answer, therefore, is: The race has tried that. All progress from that barbarous day to the present time has resulted from its displacement. Not evil, but good, has come to the race from the accumulation of wealth by those who have the ability and energy that produce it. But even if we admit for a moment that it might be better for the race to discard its present foundation, Individualism, — that it is a nobler ideal that man should labor, not for himself alone, but in and for a brotherhood of his fellows, and share with them all in common, realizing Swedenborg's idea of Heaven, where, as he says, the angels derive their happiness, not from laboring for self, but for each other, — even admit all this, and a sufficient answer is, This is not evolution, but revolution. It necessitates the changing of human nature itself — a work of aeons, even if it were good to change it, which we cannot know. It is not practicable in our day or in our age. Even if desirable theoretically, it belongs to another and long-succeeding sociological stratum. Our duty is with what is practicable now; with the next step possible in our day and generation. It is criminal to waste our energies in endeavoring to uproot, when all we can profitably or possibly accomplish is to bend the universal tree of humanity a little in the direction most favorable to the production of good fruit under existing circumstances. We might as well urge the destruction of the highest existing type of man because he failed to reach our ideal as to favor the destruction of Individualism, Private Property, the Law of Accumulation of Wealth, and the Law of Competition; for these are the highest results of human experience, the soil in which society so far has produced the best fruit. Unequally or unjustly, perhaps, as these laws sometimes operate, and imperfect as they appear to the Idealist, they are, nevertheless, like the highest type of man, the best and most valuable of all that humanity has yet accomplished.

We start, then, with a condition of affairs under which the best interests of the race are promoted, but which inevitably gives wealth to the few. Thus far, accepting conditions as they exist, the situation can be surveyed and pronounced good. The question then arises, — and, if the foregoing be correct, it is the only question with which we have to deal, — What is the proper mode of administering wealth after the laws upon which civilization is founded have thrown it into the hands of the few? And it is of this great question that I believe I offer the true solution. It will be understood that *fortunes* are here spoken of, not moderate sums saved by many years of effort, the returns from which are required for the comfortable maintenance and education of families. This is not *wealth,* but only *competence,* which it should be the aim of all to acquire.

There are but three modes in which surplus wealth can be disposed of. It can be left to the families of the decedents; or it can be bequeathed for public purposes; or, finally, it can be administered during their lives by its possessors. Under the first and second modes most of the wealth of the world that has reached the few has hitherto been applied. Let us in turn consider each of these modes. The first is the most injudicious. In monarchical countries, the estates and the greatest portion of the wealth are left to the first son, that the vanity of the parent may be gratified by the thought that his name and title are to descend to succeeding generations unimpaired. The condition of this class in Europe to-day teaches the futility of such hopes or ambitions. The successors have become impoverished through their follies or from the fall in the value of land. Even in Great Britain the strict law of entail has been found inadequate to maintain the status of an hereditary class. Its soil is rapidly passing into the hands of the stranger. Under republican institutions the division of property among the children is much fairer, but the question which forces itself upon thoughtful men in all lands is: Why should men leave great fortunes to their children? If this is done from affection, is it not misguided affection? Observation teaches that, generally speaking, it is not well for the children that they should be so burdened. Neither is it well for the

state. Beyond providing for the wife and daughters moderate sources of income, and very moderate allowances indeed, if any, for the sons, men may well hesitate, for it is no longer questionable that great sums bequeathed oftener work more for the injury than for the good of the recipients. Wise men will soon conclude that, for the best interests of the members of their families and of the state, such bequests are an improper use of their means.

It is not suggested that men who have failed to educate their sons to earn a livelihood shall cast them adrift in poverty. If any man has seen fit to rear his sons with a view to their living idle lives, or, what is highly commendable, has instilled in them the sentiment that they are in a position to labor for public ends without reference to pecuniary considerations, then, of course, the duty of the parent is to see that such are provided for *in moderation.* There are instances of millionaires' sons unspoiled by wealth, who, being rich, still perform great services in the community. Such are the very salt of the earth, as valuable as, unfortunately, they are rare; still it is not the exception, but the rule, that men must regard, and, looking at the usual result of enormous sums conferred upon legatees, the thoughtful man must shortly say, "I would as soon leave to my son a curse as the almighty dollar," and admit to himself that it is not the welfare of the children, but family pride, which inspires these enormous legacies.

As to the second mode, that of leaving wealth at death for public uses, it may be said that this is only a means for the disposal of wealth, provided a man is content to wait until he is dead before it becomes of much good in the world. Knowledge of the results of legacies bequeathed is not calculated to inspire the brightest hopes of much posthumous good being accomplished. The cases are not few in which the real object sought by the testator is not attained, nor are they few in which his real wishes are thwarted. In many cases the bequests are so used as to become only monuments of his folly. It is well to remember that it requires the exercise of not less ability than that which acquired the wealth to use it so as to be really beneficial to the community. Besides this, it may fairly be said that no man is to be extolled for doing what he cannot help doing, nor is he to be thanked by the community to which he only leaves wealth at death. Men who leave vast sums in this way may fairly be thought men who would not have left it at all, had they been able to take it with them. The memories of such cannot be held in grateful remembrance, for there is no grace in their gifts. It is not to be wondered at that such bequests seem so generally to lack the blessing.

The growing disposition to tax more and more heavily large estates left at death is a cheering indication of the growth of a salutary change in public opinion. The State of Pennsylvania now takes — subject to some exceptions — one-tenth of the property left by its citizens. The budget presented in the British Parliament the other day proposes to increase the death-duties; and, most significant of all, the new tax is to be a graduated one. Of all forms of taxation, this seems the wisest. Men who continue hoarding great sums all their lives, the proper use of which for public ends would work good to the community, should be made to feel that the community, in the form of the state, cannot thus be deprived of its proper share. By taxing estates heavily at death the state marks its condemnation of the selfish millionaire's unworthy life.

It is desirable that nations should go much further in this direction. Indeed, it is difficult to set bounds to the share of a rich man's estate which should go at his death to the public through the agency of the state, and by all means such taxes should be graduated, beginning at nothing upon moderate sums to dependents, and increasing rapidly as the amounts swell, until of the millionaire's hoard, as of Shylock's, at least

> "———The other half
> Comes to the privy coffer of the state."

This policy would work powerfully to induce the rich man to attend to the administration of wealth during his life, which is the end that society should always have in view, as being that by far most fruitful for the people. Nor need it be feared that this policy would sap the root of enterprise and render men less anxious to accumulate, for to the class whose ambition it is to leave great fortunes and be talked about after their death, it will attract even more attention, and, indeed, be a somewhat nobler ambition to have enormous sums paid over to the state from their fortunes.

There remains, then, only one mode of using great fortunes; but in this we have the true antidote for the temporary unequal distribution of wealth, the reconciliation of the rich and the poor — a reign of harmony — another ideal, differing, indeed, from that of the Communist in requiring only the further evolution of existing conditions, not the total overthrow of our civilization. It is founded upon the present most intense individualism, and the race is prepared to put it in practice by degrees whenever it pleases. Under its sway we shall have an ideal state, in which the surplus wealth of the few will become, in the best sense, the property of the many, because administered for the common good, and this wealth, passing through the hands of the few, can be made a much more potent force for the elevation of our race than if it had been distributed in small sums to the people themselves. Even the poorest can be made to see this, and to agree that great sums gathered by some of their fellow-citizens and spent for public purposes, from which the masses reap the principal benefit, are more valuable to them than if scattered among them through the course of many years in trifling amounts.

If we consider what results flow from the Cooper Institute, for instance, to the best portion of the race in New York not possessed of means, and compare these with those which would have arisen for the good of the masses from an equal sum distributed by Mr. Cooper in his lifetime in the form of wages, which is the highest form of distribution, being for work done and not for charity, we can form some estimate of the possibilities for the improvement of the race which lie embedded in the present law of the accumulation of wealth. Much of this sum, if distributed in small quantities among the people, would have been wasted in the indulgence of appetite, some of it in excess, and it may be doubted whether even the part put to the best use, that of adding to the comforts of the home, would have yielded results for the race, as a race, at all comparable to those which are flowing and are to flow from the Cooper Institute from generation to generation. Let the advocate of violent or radical change ponder well this thought.

We might even go so far as to take another instance, that of Mr. Tilden's bequest of five millions of dollars for a free library in the city of New York, but in referring to this one cannot help saying involuntarily, How much better if Mr. Tilden had devoted the last years of his own life to the proper administration of this immense sum; in which case neither legal contest nor any other cause of delay could have interfered with his aims. But let us assume that Mr. Tilden's millions finally became the means of giving to this city a noble public library, where the treasures of the world contained in books will be open to all forever, without money and without price. Considering the good of that part of the race which congregates in and around Manhattan Island, would its permanent benefit have been better promoted had these millions been allowed to circulate in small sums through the hands of the masses? Even the most strenuous advocate of Communism must entertain a doubt upon this subject. Most of those who think will probably entertain no doubt whatever.

Poor and restricted are our opportunities in this life; narrow our horizon; our best work most imperfect; but rich men should be thankful for one inestimable boon. They have it in their power during their lives to busy themselves in organizing benefactions from which the masses of their fellows will derive lasting advantage, and thus dignify their own lives. The highest life is probably to be reached, not by such imitation of the life of Christ as Count Tolstoï gives us, but, while animated by Christ's spirit, by recognizing the changed conditions of this age, and adopting modes of expressing this spirit suitable to the changed conditions under which we live; still laboring for the good of our fellows, which was the essence of his life and teaching, but laboring in a different manner.

This, then, is held to be the duty of the man of Wealth: First, to set an example of modest, unostentatious living, shunning display or extravagance; to provide moderately for the legitimate wants of those dependent upon him; and after doing so to consider all surplus revenues which come to him simply as trust funds, which he is called upon to administer, and strictly bound as a matter of duty to administer in the manner which, in his judgment, is best calculated to produce the most beneficial results for the community — the man of wealth thus becoming the mere agent and trustee for his poorer brethren, bringing to their service his superior wisdom, experience, and ability to administer, doing for them better than they would or could do for themselves.

We are met here with the difficulty of determining what are moderate sums to leave to members of the family; what is modest, unostentatious living; what is the test of extravagance. There must be different standards for different conditions. The answer is that it is as impossible to name exact amounts or actions as it is to define good manners, good taste, or the rules of propriety; but, nevertheless, these are verities, well known although undefinable. Public sentiment is quick to know and to feel what offends these. So in the case of wealth. The rule in regard to good taste in the dress of men or women applies here. Whatever makes one conspicuous offends the canon. If any family be chiefly known for display, for extravagance in home, table, equipage, for enormous sums ostentatiously spent in any form upon itself, — if these be its chief distinctions, we have no difficulty in estimating its nature or culture. So likewise in regard to the use or abuse of its surplus wealth, or to generous, freehanded coöperation in good public uses, or to unabated efforts to accumulate and hoard to the last, whether they administer or bequeath. The verdict rests with

the best and most enlightened public sentiment. The community will surely judge, and its judgments will not often be wrong.

The best uses to which surplus wealth can be put have already been indicated. Those who would administer wisely must, indeed, be wise, for one of the serious obstacles to the improvement of our race is indiscriminate charity. It were better for mankind that the millions of the rich were thrown into the sea than so spent as to encourage the slothful, the drunken, the unworthy. Of every thousand dollars spent in so called charity today, it is probable that $950 is unwisely spent; so spent, indeed, as to produce the very evils which it proposes to mitigate or cure. A wellknown writer of philosophic books admitted the other day that he had given a quarter of a dollar to a man who approached him as he was coming to visit the house of his friend. He knew nothing of the habits of this beggar; knew not the use that would be made of this money, although he had every reason to suspect that it would be spent improperly. This man professed to be a disciple of Herbert Spencer; yet the quarter-dollar given that night will probably work more injury than all the money which its thoughtless donor will ever be able to give in true charity will do good. He only gratified his own feelings, saved himself from annoyance, — and this was probably one of the most selfish and very worst actions of his life, for in all respects he is most worthy.

In bestowing charity, the main consideration should be to help those who will help themselves; to provide part of the means by which those who desire to improve may do so; to give those who desire to rise the aids by which they may rise; to assist, but rarely or never to do all. Neither the individual nor the race is improved by alms-giving. Those worthy of assistance, except in rare cases, seldom require assistance. The really valuable men of the race never do, except in cases of accident or sudden change. Every one has, of course, cases of individuals brought to his own knowledge where temporary assistance can do genuine good, and these he will not overlook. But the amount which can be wisely given by the individual for individuals is necessarily limited by his lack of knowledge of the circumstances connected with each. He is the only true reformer who is as careful and as anxious not to aid the unworthy as he is to aid the worthy, and, perhaps, even more so, for in alms-giving more injury is probably done by rewarding vice than by relieving virtue.

The rich man is thus almost restricted to following the examples of Peter Cooper, Enoch Pratt of Baltimore, Mr. Pratt of Brooklyn, Senator Stanford, and others, who know that the best means of benefiting the community is to place within its reach the ladders upon which the aspiring can rise — parks, and means of recreation, by which men are helped in body and mind; works of art, certain to give pleasure and improve the public taste, and public institutions of various kinds, which will improve the general condition of the people; — in this manner returning their surplus wealth to the mass of their fellows in the forms best calculated to do them lasting good.

Thus is the problem of Rich and Poor to be solved. The laws of accumulation will be left free; the laws of distribution free. Individualism will continue, but the millionaire will be but a trustee for the poor; intrusted for a season with a great part of the increased wealth of the community, but administering it for the community far better than it could or would have done for itself. The best minds will thus have reached a stage in the development of the race in which it is clearly seen that there is no mode of disposing of surplus wealth creditable to thoughtful and earnest men into whose hands it flows save by using it year by year for the general good. This day already dawns. But a little while, and although, without incurring the pity of their fellows, men may die sharers in great business enterprises from which their capital cannot be or has not been withdrawn, and is left chiefly at death for public uses, yet the man who dies leaving behind him millions of available wealth, which was his to administer during life, will pass away "unwept, unhonored, and unsung," no matter to what uses he leaves the dross which he cannot take with him. Of such as these the public verdict will then be: "The man who dies thus rich dies disgraced."

Such, in my opinion, is the true Gospel concerning Wealth, obedience to which is destined some day to solve the problem of the Rich and the Poor, and to bring "Peace on earth, among men Good-Will."

Walt Whitman: DEMOCRATIC VISTAS

AS the greatest lessons of Nature through the universe are perhaps the lessons of variety and freedom, the same present the greatest lessons also in New World politics and progress. If a man were ask'd, for instance, the distinctive points contrasting modern European and American political and other life with the old Asiatic cultus, as lingering-bequeath'd yet in China and Turkey, he might find the amount of them in John Stuart Mill's profound essay on Liberty in the future, where he demands two main constituents, or substrata, for a truly grand nationality — 1st, a large variety of character — and 2d, full play for human nature to expand itself in numberless and even conflicting directions — (seems to be for general humanity much like the influences that make up, in their limitless field, that perennial health-action of the air we call the weather — an infinite number of currents and forces, and contributions, and temperatures, and cross purposes, whose ceaseless play of counterpart upon counterpart brings constant restoration and vitality.) With this thought — and not for itself alone, but all it necessitates, and draws after it — let me begin my speculations.

America, filling the present with greatest deeds and problems, cheerfully accepting the past, including feudalism, (as, indeed, the present is but the legitimate birth of the past, including feudalism), counts, as I reckon, for her justification and success, (for who, as yet, dare claim success?) almost entirely on the future. Nor is that hope unwarranted. Today, ahead, though dimly yet, we see, in vistas, a copious, sane, gigantic offspring. For our New World I consider far less important for what it has done, or what it is, than for results to come. Sole among nationalities, these States have assumed the task to put in forms of lasting power and practicality, on areas of amplitude rivaling the operations of the physical kosmos, the moral political speculations of ages, long, long deferr'd, the democratic republican principle, and the theory of development and perfection by voluntary standards, and self-reliance. Who else, indeed, except the United States, in history, so far, have accepted in unwitting faith, and, as we now see, stand, act upon, and go security for, these things?

But preluding no longer, let me strike the key-note of the following strain. First premising that, though the passages of it have been written at widely different times, (it is, in fact, a collection of memoranda, perhaps for future designers, comprehenders,) and though it may be open to the charge of one part contradicting another — for there are opposite sides to the great question of democracy, as to every great question — I feel the parts harmoniously blended in my own realization and convictions, and present them to be read only in such oneness, each page and each claim and assertion modified and temper'd by the others. Bear in

Reprinted from *Democratic Vistas, and Other Papers* (London: Walter Scott, 1888), pp. 1–37.

mind, too, that they are not the result of studying up in political economy, but of the ordinary sense, observing, wandering among men, these States, these stirring years of war and peace. I will not gloss over the appalling dangers of universal suffrage in the United States. In fact, it is to admit and face these dangers I am writing. To him or her within whose thought rages the battle, advancing, retreating, between democracy's convictions, aspirations, and the people's crudeness, vice, caprices, I mainly write this essay. I shall use the words America and democracy as convertible terms. Not an ordinary one is the issue. The United States are destined either to surmount the gorgeous history of feudalism, or else prove the most tremendous failure of time. Not the least doubtful am I on any prospects of their material success. The triumphant future of their business, geographic and productive departments, on larger scales and in more varieties than ever, is certain. In those respects the republic must soon (if she does not already) outstrip all examples hitherto afforded, and dominate the world.

Admitting all this, with the priceless value of our political institutions, general suffrage, (and fully acknowledging the latest, widest opening of the doors,) I say that, far deeper than these, what finally and only is to make of our western world a nationality superior to any hitherto known, and outtopping the past, must be vigorous, yet unsuspected Literatures, perfect personalities and sociologies, original, transcendental, and expressing (what, in highest sense, are not yet express'd at all,) democracy and the modern. With these, and out of these, I promulgate new races of Teachers, and of perfect Women, indispensable to endow the birth-stock of a New World. For feudalism, caste, the ecclesiastic tradi-

tions, though palpably retreating from political institutions, still hold essentially, by their spirit, even in this country, entire possession of the more important fields, indeed the very subsoil, of education, and of social standards and literature.

I say that democracy can never prove itself beyond cavil, until it founds and luxuriantly grows its own forms of art, poems, schools, theology, displacing all that exists, or that has been produced anywhere in the past, under opposite influences. It is curious to me that while so many voices, pens, minds, in the press, lecture-rooms, in our Congress, &c., are discussing intellectual topics, pecuniary dangers, legislative problems, the suffrage, tariff and labor questions, and the various business and benevolent needs of America, with propositions, remedies, often worth deep attention, there is one need, a hiatus the profoundest, that no eye seems to perceive, no voice to state. Our fundamental want to-day in the United States, with closest, amplest reference to present conditions, and to the future, is of a class, and the clear idea of a class, of native authors, literatuses, far different, far higher in grade than any yet known, sacerdotal, modern, fit to cope with our occasions, lands, permeating the whole mass of American mentality, taste, belief, breathing into it a new breath of life, giving it decision, affecting politics far more than the popular superficial suffrage, with results inside and underneath the elections of Presidents or Congresses — radiating, begetting appropriate teachers, schools, manners, and, as its grandest result, accomplishing, (what neither the schools nor the churches and their clergy have hitherto accomplish'd, and without which this nation will no more stand, permanently, soundly, than a house will stand without a substratum,) a religious and moral character beneath the political and productive and intellectual bases of the States. For know you not, dear, earnest reader, that the people of our land may all read and write, and may all possess the right to vote — and yet the main things may be entirely lacking? — (and this to suggest them.)

View'd, to-day, from a point of view sufficiently over-arching, the problem of humanity all over the civilized world is social and religious, and is to be finally met and treated by literature. The priest departs, and the divine literatus comes. Never was anything more wanted than, to-day, and here in the States, the poet of the modern is wanted, or the great literatus of the modern. At all times, perhaps, the central point in any nation, and that whence it is itself really sway'd the most, and whence it sways others, is its national literature, especially its archetypal poems. Above all previous lands, a great original literature is surely to become the justification and reliance, (in some respects the sole reliance,) of American democracy.

Few are aware how the great literature penetrates all, gives hue to all, shapes aggregates and individuals, and, after subtle ways, with irresistible power, constructs, sustains, demolishes at will. Why tower, in reminiscence, above all the nations of the earth, two special lands, petty in themselves, yet inexpressibly gigantic, beautiful, columnar? Immortal Judah lives, and Greece immortal lives, in a couple of poems.

Nearer than this. It is not generally realized, but it is true, as the genius of Greece, and all the sociology, personality, politics and religion of those wonderful states, resided in their literature or esthetics, that what was afterwards the main support of European chivalry, the feudal, ecclesiastical, dynastic world over

there — forming its osseous structure, holding it together for hundreds, thousands of years, preserving its flesh and bloom, giving it form, decision, rounding it out, and so saturating it in the conscious and unconscious blood, breed, belief, and intuitions of men, that it still prevails powerful to this day, in defiance of the mighty changes of time — was its literature, permeating to the very marrow, especially that major part, its enchanting songs, ballads, and poems.

To the ostent of the senses and eyes, I know, the influences which stamp the world's history are wars, uprisings or downfalls of dynasties, changeful movements of trade, important inventions, navigation, military or civil governments, advent of powerful personalities, conquerors, &c. These of course play their part; yet, it may be, a single new thought, imagination, abstract principle, even literary style, fit for the time, put in shape by some great literatus, and projected among mankind, may duly cause changes, growths, removals, greater than the longest and bloodiest war, or the most stupendous merely political, dynastic, or commercial overturn.

In short, as, though it may not be realized, it is strictly true, that a few first-class poets, philosophs, and authors, have substantially settled and given status to the entire religion, education, law, sociology, &c., of the hitherto civilized world, by tinging and often creating the atmospheres out of which they have arisen, such also must stamp, and more than ever stamp, the interior and real democratic construction of this American continent, to-day, and days to come. Remember also this fact of difference, that, while through the antique and through the mediaeval ages, highest thoughts and ideals realized themselves, and their expression made its way by other arts, as much as, or even more than by, technical literature, (not open to the mass of persons, or even to the majority of eminent persons,) such literature in our day and for current purposes, is not only more eligible than all the other arts put together, but has become the only general means of morally influencing the world. Painting, sculpture, and the dramatic theatre, it would seem, no longer play an indispensable or even important part in the workings and mediumship of intellect, utility, or even high esthetics. Architecture remains, doubtless with capacities, and a real future. Then music, the combiner, nothing more spiritual, nothing more sensuous, a god, yet completely human, advances, prevails, holds highest place; supplying in certain wants and quarters what nothing else could supply. Yet in the civilization of to-day it is undeniable that, over all the arts, literature dominates, serves beyond all — shapes the character of church and school — or, at any rate, is capable of doing so. Including the literature of science, its scope is indeed unparallel'd.

Before proceeding further, it were perhaps well to discriminate on certain points. Literature tills its crops in many fields, and some may flourish, while others lag. What I say in these Vistas has its main bearing on imaginative literature, especially poetry, the stock of all. In the department of science, and the specialty of journalism, there appear, in these States, promises, perhaps fulfilments, of highest earnestness, reality, and life. These, of course, are modern. But in the region of imaginative, spinal and essential attributes, something equivalent to creation is, for our age and lands, imperatively demanded. For not only is it not enough that the new blood, new frame of democracy shall be vivified and held together merely by political means,

superficial suffrage, legislation, &c., but it is clear to me that, unless it goes deeper, gets at least as firm and as warm a hold in men's hearts, emotions and belief, as, in their days, feudalism or ecclesiasticism, and inaugurates its own perennial sources, welling from the centre forever, its strength will be defective, its growth doubtful, and its main charm wanting. I suggest, therefore, the possibility, should some two or three really original American poets, (perhaps artists or lecturers,) arise, mounting the horizon like planets, stars of the first magnitude, that, from their eminence, fusing contributions, races, far localities, &c., together, they would give more compaction and more moral identity, (the quality today most needed,) to the States, than all its Constitutions, legislative and judicial ties, and all its hitherto political, warlike, or materialistic expériences. As, for instance, there could hardly happen anything that would more serve the States, with all their variety of origins, their diverse climes, cities, standards, &c., than possessing an aggregate of heroes, characters, exploits, sufferings, prosperity or misfortune, glory or disgrace, common to all, typical of all — no less, but even greater would it be to possess the aggregation of a cluster of mighty poets, artists, teachers, fit for us, national expressers, comprehending and effusing for the men and women of the States, what is universal, native, common to all, inland and seaboard, northern and southern. The historians say of ancient Greece, with her ever-jealous autonomies, cities, and states, that the only positive unity she ever own'd or receiv'd, was the sad unity of a common subjection, at the last, to foreign conquerors. Subjection, aggregation of that sort, is impossible to America; but the fear of conflicting and irreconcilable interiors, and the lack of a common skeleton, knitting all close, continually haunts me. Or, if it does not, nothing is plainer than the need, a long period to come, of a fusion of the States into the only reliable identity, the moral and artistic one. For, I say, the true nationality of the States, the genuine union, when we come to a mortal crisis, is, and is to be, after all, neither the written law, nor, (as is generally supposed,) either self-interest, or common pecuniary or material objects — but the fervid and tremendous IDEA, melting everything else with resistless heat, and solving all lesser and definite distinctions in vast, indefinite, spiritual, emotional power.

It may be claim'd, (and I admit the weight of the claim,) that common and general worldly prosperity, and a populace well-to-do, and with all life's material comforts, is the main thing, and is enough. It may be argued that our republic is, in performance, really enacting to-day the grandest arts, poems, &c., by beating up the wilderness into fertile farms, and in her railroads, ships, machinery, &c. And it may be ask'd, Are these not better, indeed, for America, than any utterances even of greatest rhapsode, artist, or literatus?

I too hail those achievements with pride and joy: then answer that the soul of man will not with such only — nay, not with such at all — be finally satisfied; but needs what, (standing on these and on all things, as the feet stand on the ground,) is address'd to the loftiest, to itself alone.

Out of such considerations, such truths, arises for treatment in these Vistas the important question of character, of an American stock-personality, with literatures and arts for outlets and return-expressions, and, of course, to correspond, within outlines common to all. To these, the main affair, the thinkers of the United States, in general so acute, have either given feeblest attention, or have remain'd, and remain, in a state of somnolence.

For my part, I would alarm and caution even the political and business reader, and to the utmost extent, against the prevailing delusion that the establishment of free political institutions, and plentiful intellectual smartness, with general good order, physical plenty, industry, &c., (desirable and precious advantages as they all are,) do, of themselves, determine and yield to our experiment of democracy the fruitage of success. With such advantages at present fully, or almost fully, possess'd — the Union just issued, victorious, from the struggle with the only foes it need ever fear, (namely, those within itself, the interior ones,) and with unprecedented materialistic advancement — society, in these States, is canker'd, crude, superstitious, and rotten. Political, or law-made society is, and private, or voluntary society, is also. In any vigor, the element of the moral conscience, the most important, the verteber to State or man, seems to me either entirely lacking, or seriously enfeebled or ungrown.

I say we had best look our times and lands searchingly in the face, like a physician diagnosing some deep disease. Never was there, perhaps, more hollowness at heart than at present, and here in the United States. Genuine belief seems to have left us. The underlying principles of the States are not honestly believ'd in, (for all this hectic glow, and these melo-dramatic screamings,) nor is humanity itself believ'd in. What penetrating eye does not everywhere see through the mask? The spectacle is appalling. We live in an atmosphere of hypocrisy throughout. The men believe not in the women, nor the women in the men. A scornful superciliousness rules in literature. The aim of all the *littérateurs* is to find something to make fun of. A lot of churches, sects, &c., the most dismal phantasms I know, usurp the name of religion. Conversation is a mass of badinage. From deceit in the spirit, the mother of all false deeds, the offspring is already incalculable. An acute and candid person, in the revenue department in Washington, who is led by the course of his employment to regularly visit the cities, north, south and west, to investigate frauds, has talk'd much with me about his discoveries. The depravity of the business classes of our country is not less than has been supposed, but infinitely greater. The official services of America, national, state, and municipal, in all their branches and departments, except the judiciary, are saturated in corruption, bribery, falsehood, mal-administration; and the judiciary is tainted. The great cities reek with respectable as much as non-respectable robbery and scoundrelism. In fashionable life, flippancy, tepid amours, weak infidelism, small aims, or no aims at all, only to kill time. In business, (this all-devouring modern word, business,) the one sole object is, by any means, pecuniary gain. The magician's serpent in the fable ate up all the other serpents; and money-making is our magician's serpent, remaining to-day sole master of the field. The best class we show, is but a mob of fashionably dress'd speculators and vulgarians. True, indeed, behind this fantastic farce, enacted on the visible stage of society, solid things and stupendous labors are to be discover'd, existing crudely and going on in the background, to advance and tell themselves in time. Yet the truths are none the less terrible. I say that our New World democracy, however great a success in uplifting the masses out of their sloughs, in materialistic development, products, and in a certain highly-deceptive superficial popular intellectuality, is, so far, an almost complete failure in its social aspects, and in really grand religious, moral, literary, and esthetic results. In vain do we march with unprecedented strides to empire so colossal, outvying the antique, beyond Alexander's, beyond the proudest sway of Rome. In vain have we annex'd Texas, California, Alaska, and reach north for Canada and south for Cuba. It is as if we were somehow being endow'd with a vast and more and more thoroughly-appointed body, and then left with little or no soul.

Let me illustrate further, as I write, with current observations, localities, &c. The subject is important, and will bear repetition. After an absence, I am now again (September, 1870) in New York City and Brooklyn, on a few weeks' vacation. The splendor, picturesqueness, and oceanic amplitude and rush of these great cities, the unsurpass'd situation, rivers and bay, sparkling sea-tides, costly and lofty new buildings, façades of marble and iron, of original grandeur and elegance of design, with the masses of gay color, the preponderance of white and blue, the flags flying, the endless ships, the tumultuous streets, Broadway, the heavy, low, musical roar, hardly ever intermitted, even at night; the jobbers' houses, the rich shops, the wharves, the great Central Park, and the Brooklyn Park of hills, (as I wander among them this beautiful fall weather, musing, watching, absorbing) — the assemblages of the citizens in their groups, conversations, trades, evening amusements, or along the by-quarters — these, I say, and the like of these, completely satisfy my senses of power, fulness, motion, &c., and give me, through such senses and appetites, and through my esthetic conscience, a continued exaltation and absolute fulfilment. Always and more and more, as I cross the East and North rivers, the ferries, or with the pilots in their pilot-houses, or pass an hour in Wall street, or the gold exchange, I realize, (if we must admit such partialisms,) that not Nature alone is great in her fields of freedom and the open air, in her storms, the shows of night and day, the mountains, forests, seas — but in the artificial, the work of man too is equally great — in this profusion of teeming humanity — in these ingenuities, streets, goods, houses, ships — these hurrying, feverish, electric crowds of men, their complicated business genius, (not least among the geniuses,) and all this mighty, many-threaded wealth and industry concentrated here.

But sternly discarding, shutting our eyes to the glow and grandeur of the general superficial effect, coming down to what is of the only real importance, Personalities, and examining minutely, we question, we ask, Are there, indeed, *men* here worthy the name? Are there athletes? Are there perfect women, to match the generous material luxuriance? Is there a pervading atmosphere of beautiful manners? Are there crops of fine youths, and majestic old persons? Are there arts worthy freedom and a rich people? Is there a great moral and religious civilization — the only justification of a great material one? Confess that to severe eyes, using the moral microscope upon humanity, a sort of dry and flat Sahara appears, these cities, crowded with petty grotesques, malformations, phantoms, playing meaningless antics. Confess that everywhere, in shop, street, church, theatre, bar-room, official chair, are pervading flippancy and vulgarity, low cunning, infidelity — everywhere the

youth puny, impudent, foppish, prematurely ripe — everywhere an abnormal libidinousness, unhealthy forms, male, female, painted, padded, dyed, chignon'd, muddy complexions, bad blood, the capacity for good motherhood deceasing or deceas'd, shallow notions of beauty, with a range of manners, or rather lack of manners, (considering the advantages enjoy'd,) probably the meanest to be seen in the world.

Of all this, and these lamentable conditions, to breathe into them the breath recuperative of sane and heroic life, I say a new founded literature, not merely to copy and reflect existing surfaces, or pander to what is called taste — not only to amuse, pass away time, celebrate the beautiful, the refined, the past, or exhibit technical, rhythmic, or grammatical dexterity — but a literature underlying life, religious, consistent with science, handling the elements and forces with competent power, teaching and training men — and, as perhaps the most precious of its results, achieving the entire redemption of woman out of these incredible holds and webs of silliness, millinery, and every kind of dyspeptic depletion — and thus insuring to the States a strong and sweet Female Race, a race of perfect Mothers — is what is needed.

And now, in the full conception of these facts and points, and all that they infer, pro and con — with yet unshaken faith in the elements of the American masses, the composites, of both sexes, and even consider'd as individuals — and ever recognizing in them the broadest bases of the best literary and esthetic appreciation — I proceed with my speculations, Vistas.

First, let us see what we can make out of a brief, general, sentimental consideration of political democracy, and whence it has arisen, with regard to some of its current features, as an aggregate, and as the basic structure of our future literature and authorship. We shall, it is true, quickly and continually find the origin-idea of the singleness of man, individualism, asserting itself, and cropping forth, even from the opposite ideas. But the mass, or lump character, for imperative reasons, is to be ever carefully weigh'd, borne in mind, and provided for. Only from it, and from its proper regulation and potency, comes the other, comes the chance of individualism. The two are contradictory, but our task is to reconcile them.

The political history of the past may be summ'd up as having grown out of what underlies the words, order, safety, caste, and especially out of the need of some prompt deciding authority, and of cohesion at all cost. Leaping time, we come to the period within the memory of people now living, when, as from some lair where they had slumber'd long, accumulating wrath, sprang up and are yet active, (1790, and on even to the present, 1870,) those noisy eructations, destructive iconoclasms, a fierce sense of wrongs, amid which moves the form, well known in modern history, in the old world, stain'd with much blood, and mark'd by savage reactionary clamors and demands. These bear, mostly, as on one inclosing point of need.

For after the rest is said — after the many time-honor'd and really true things for subordination, experience, rights of property, &c., have been listen'd to and acquiesced in — after the valuable and well-settled statement of our duties and relations in society is thoroughly conn'd over and exhausted — it remains to bring forward and modify everything else with the idea of that Something a man is, (last precious consolation of the drudging poor,) standing apart from all else, di-

vine in his own right and a woman in hers, sole and untouchable by any canons of authority, or any rule derived from precedent, state-safety, the acts of legislatures, or even from what is called religion, modesty, or art. The radiation of this truth is the key of the most significant doings of our immediately preceding three centuries, and has been the political genesis and life of America. Advancing visibly, it still more advances invisibly. Underneath the fluctuations of the expressions of society, as well as the movements of the politics of the leading nations of the world, we see steadily pressing ahead and strengthening itself, even in the midst of immense tendencies toward aggregation, this image of completeness in separatism, of individual personal dignity, of a single person, either male or female, characterized in the main, not from extrinsic acquirements or position, but in the pride of himself or herself alone; and, as an eventual conclusion and summing up, (or else the entire scheme of things is aimless, a cheat, a crash,) the simple idea that the last, best dependence is to be upon humanity itself, and its own inherent, normal, full-grown qualities, without any superstitious support whatever. This idea of perfect individualism it is indeed that deepest tinges and gives character to the idea of the aggregate. For it is mainly or altogether to serve independent separatism that we favor a strong generalization, consolidation. As it is to give the best vitality and freedom to the rights of the States, (every bit as important as the right of nationality, the union,) that we insist on the identity of the Union at all hazards.

The purpose of democracy — supplanting old belief in the necessary absoluteness of establish'd dynastic rulership, temporal, ecclesiastical, and scholastic, as furnishing the only security against chaos, crime, and ignorance — is, through many transmigrations, and amid endless ridicules, arguments, and ostensible failures, to illustrate, at all hazards, this doctrine or theory that man, properly train'd in sanest, highest freedom, may and must become a law, and series of laws, unto himself, surrounding and providing for, not only his own personal control, but all his relations to other individuals, and to the State; and that, while other theories, as in the past histories of nations, have proved wise enough, and indispensable perhaps for their conditions, *this,* as matters now stand in our civilized world, is the only scheme worth working from, as warranting results like those of Nature's laws, reliable, when once establish'd, to carry on themselves.

The argument of the matter is extensive, and, we admit, by no means all on one side. What we shall offer will be far, far from sufficient. But while leaving unsaid much that should properly even prepare the way for the treatment of this many-sided question of political liberty, equality, or republicanism — leaving the whole history and consideration of the feudal plan and its products, embodying humanity, its politics and civilization, through the retrospect of past time, (which plan and products, indeed, make up all of the past, and a large part of the present) — leaving unanswer'd, at least by any specific and local answer, many a well-wrought argument and instance, and many a conscientious declamatory cry and warning — as, very lately, from an eminent and venerable person abroad — things, problems, full of doubt, dread, suspense, (not new to me, but old occupiers of many an anxious hour in city's din, or night's silence,) we still may give a page or so, whose drift is opportune. Time alone can finally answer these

things. But as a substitute in passing, let us, even if fragmentarily, throw forth a short direct or indirect suggestion of the premises of that other plan, in the new spirit, under the new forms, started here in our America.

As to the political section of Democracy, which introduces and breaks ground for further and vaster sections, few probably are the minds, even in these republican States, that fully comprehend the aptness of that phrase, "THE GOVERNMENT OF THE PEOPLE, BY THE PEOPLE, FOR THE PEOPLE," which we inherit from the lips of Abraham Lincoln; a formula whose verbal shape is homely wit, but whose scope includes both the totality and all minutiae of the lesson.

The People! Like our huge earth itself, which, to ordinary scansion, is full of vulgar contradictions and offence, man, viewed in the lump, displeases, and is a constant puzzle and affront to the merely educated classes. The rare, cosmical, artist-mind, lit with the Infinite, alone confronts his manifold and oceanic qualities — but taste, intelligence and culture, (so-called,) have been against the masses, and remain so. There is plenty of glamour about the most damnable crimes and hoggish meannesses, special and general, of the feudal and dynastic world over there, with its *personnel* of lords and queens and courts, so well-dress'd and so handsome. But the People are ungrammatical, untidy, and their sins gaunt and ill-bred.

Literature, strictly consider'd, has never recognized the People, and, whatever may be said, does not to-day. Speaking generally, the tendencies of literature, as hitherto pursued, have been to make mostly critical and querulous men. It seems as if, so far, there were some natural repugnance between a literary and professional life, and the rude rank spirit of the democracies. There is, in later literature, a treatment of benevolence, a charity business, rife enough it is true; but I know nothing more rare, even in this country, than a fit scientific estimate and reverent appreciation of the People — of their measureless wealth of latent power and capacity, their vast, artistic contrasts of lights and shades — with, in America, their entire reliability in emergencies, and a certain breadth of historic grandeur, of peace or war, far surpassing all the vaunted samples of book-heroes, or any *haut ton* coteries, in all the records of the world.

The movements of the late secession war, and their results, to any sense that studies well and comprehends them, show that popular democracy, whatever its faults and dangers, practically justifies itself beyond the proudest claims and wildest hopes of its enthusiasts. Probably no future age can know, but I well know, how the gist of this fiercest and most resolute of the world's war-like contentions resided exclusively in the unnamed, unknown rank and file; and how the brunt of its labor of death was, to all essential purposes, volunteer'd. The People, of their own choice, fighting, dying for their own idea, insolently attack'd by the secession-slave-power, and its very existence imperil'd. Descending to detail, entering any of the armies, and mixing with the private soldiers, we see and have seen august spectacles. We have seen the alacrity with which the American-born populace, the peaceablest and most good-natured race in the world, and the most personally independent and intelligent, and the least fitted to submit to the irksomeness and exasperation of regimental discipline, sprang, at the first tap of the drum, to arms — not for gain, nor even glory, nor to repel invasion —

but for an emblem, a mere abstraction — for the life, *the safety of the flag.* We have seen the unequal'd docility and obedience of these soldiers. We have seen them tried long and long by hopelessness, mismanagement, and by defeat; have seen the incredible slaughter toward or through which the armies, (as at first Fredericksburg, and afterward at the Wilderness,) still unhesitatingly obey'd orders to advance. We have seen them in trench, or crouching behind breastwork, or tramping in deep mud, or amid pouring rain or thick-falling snow, or under forced marches in hottest summer (as on the road to get to Gettysburg) — vast suffocating swarms, divisions, corps, with every single man so grimed and black with sweat and dust, his own mother would not have known him — his clothes all dirty, stain'd and torn, with sour, accumulated sweat for perfume — many a comrade, perhaps a brother, sunstruck, staggering out, dying, by the roadside, of exhaustion — yet the great bulk bearing steadily on, cheery enough, hollow-bellied from hunger, but sinewy with unconquerable resolution.

We have seen this race proved by wholesale, by drearier, yet more fearful tests — the wound, the amputation, the shatter'd face or limb, the slow hot fever, long impatient anchorage in bed, and all the forms of maiming, operation and disease. Alas! America have we seen, though only in her early youth, already to hospital brought. There have we watch'd these soldiers, many of them only boys in years — mark'd their decorum, their religious nature and fortitude, and their sweet affection. Wholesale, truly. For at the front, and through the camps, in countless tents, stood the regimental, brigade and division hospitals; while everywhere amid the land, in or near cities, rose clusters of huge, white-wash'd, crowded, one-story wooden barracks; and there ruled agony with bitter scourge, yet seldom brought a cry; and there stalk'd death by day and night along the narrow aisles between the rows of cots, or by the blankets on the ground, and touch'd lightly many a poor sufferer, often with blessed, welcome touch.

I know not whether I shall be understood, but I realize that it is finally from what I learn'd personally mixing in such scenes that I am now penning these pages. One night in the gloomiest period of the war, in the Patent office hospital in Washington city, as I stood by the bedside of a Pennsylvania soldier, who lay, conscious of quick approaching death, yet perfectly calm, and with noble, spiritual manner, the veteran surgeon, turning aside, said to me, that though he had witness'd many, many deaths of soldiers, and had been a worker at Bull Run, Antietam, Fredericksburg, &c., he had not seen yet the first case of man or boy that met the approach of dissolution with cowardly qualms or terror. My own observation fully bears out the remark.

What have we here, if not, towering above all talk and argument, the plentifully-supplied, last-needed proof of democracy, in its personalities? Curiously enough, too, the proof on this point comes, I should say, every bit as much from the south, as from the north. Although I have spoken only of the latter, yet I deliberately include all. Grand, common stock! to me the accomplish'd and convincing growth, prophetic of the future; proof undeniable to sharpest sense, of perfect beauty, tenderness and pluck, that never feudal lord, nor Greek, nor Roman breed, yet rival'd. Let no tongue ever speak in disparagement of the American races, north or south, to one

who has been through the war in the great army hospitals.

Meantime, general humanity, (for to that we return, as, for our purposes, what it really is, to bear in mind,) has always, in every department, been full of perverse maleficence, and is so yet. In downcast hours the soul thinks it always will be — but soon recovers from such sickly moods. I myself see clearly enough the crude, defective streaks in all the strata of the common people; the specimens and vast collections of the ignorant, the credulous, the unfit and uncouth, the incapable, and the very low and poor. The eminent person just mention'd sneeringly asks whether we expect to elevate and improve a nation's politics by absorbing such morbid collections and qualities therein. The point is a formidable one, and there will doubtless always be numbers of solid and reflective citizens who will never get over it. Our answer is general, and is involved in the scope and letter of this essay. We believe the ulterior object of political and all other government, (having, of course, provided for the police, the safety of life, property, and for the basic statute and common law, and their administration, always first in order,) to be among the rest, not merely to rule, to repress disorder, &c., but to develop, to open up to cultivation, to encourage the possibilities of all beneficent and manly outcroppage, and of that aspiration for independence, and the pride and self-respect latent in all characters. (Or, if there be exceptions, we cannot, fixing our eyes on them alone, make theirs the rule for all.)

I say the mission of government, henceforth, in civilized lands, is not repression alone, and not authority alone, not even of law, nor by that favorite standard of the eminent writer, the rule of the best man, the born heroes and captains of the race, (as if such ever, or one time out of a hundred, get into the big places, elective or dynastic) — but higher than the highest arbitrary rule, to train communities through all their grades, beginning with individuals and ending there again, to rule themselves. What Christ appear'd for in the moral-spiritual field for human-kind, namely, that in respect to the absolute soul, there is in the possession of such by each single individual, something so transcendent, so incapable of gradations, (like life,) that, to that extent, it places all beings on a common level, utterly regardless of the distinctions of intellect, virtue, station, or any height or lowliness whatever — is tallied in like manner, in this other field, by democracy's rule that men, the nation, as a common aggregate of living identities, affording in each a separate and complete subject for freedom, worldly thrift and happiness, and for a fair chance for growth, and for protection in citizenship, &c., must, to the political extent of the suffrage or vote, if no further, be placed, in each and in the whole, on one broad, primary, universal, common platform.

The purpose is not altogether direct; perhaps it is more indirect. For it is not that democracy is of exhaustive account, in itself. Perhaps, indeed, it is, (like Nature,) of no account in itself. It is that, as we see, it is the best, perhaps only, fit and full means, formulater, general caller-forth, trainer, for the million, not for grand material personalities only, but for immortal souls. To be a voter with the rest is not so much; and this, like every institute, will have its imperfections. But to become an enfranchised man, and now, impediments removed, to stand and start without humiliation, and equal with the rest; to commence, or have the road clear'd to commence, the

grand experiment of development, whose end, (perhaps requiring several generations,) may be the forming of a full-grown man or woman — that *is* something. To ballast the State is also secured, and in our times is to be secured, in no other way.

We do not, (at any rate I do not,) put it either on the ground that the People, the masses, even the best of them, are, in their latent or exhibited qualities, essentially sensible and good — nor on the ground of their rights; but that good or bad, rights or no rights, the democratic formula is the only safe and preservative one for coming times. We endow the masses with the suffrage for their own sake, no doubt; then, perhaps still more, from another point of view, for community's sake. Leaving the rest to the sentimentalists, we present freedom as sufficient in its scientific aspect, cold as ice, reasoning, deductive, clear and passionless as crystal.

Democracy too is law, and of the strictest, amplest kind. Many suppose, (and often in its own ranks the error,) that it means a throwing aside of law, and running riot. But, briefly, it is the superior law, not alone that of physical force, the body, which, adding to, it supersedes with that of the spirit. Law is the unshakable order of the universe forever; and the law over all, and law of laws, is the law of successions; that of the superior law, in time, gradually supplanting and overwhelming the inferior one. (While, for myself, I would cheerfully agree — first covenanting that the formative tendencies shall be administer'd in favor, or at least not against it, and that this reservation be closely construed — that until the individual or community show due signs, or be so minor and fractional as not to endanger the State, the condition of authoritative tutelage may continue, and self-government must abide its time.) Nor is the esthetic point, always an important one, without fascination for highest aiming souls. The common ambition strains for elevations, to become some privileged exclusive. The master sees greatness and health in being part of the mass; nothing will do as well as common ground. Would you have in yourself the divine, vast, general law? Then merge yourself in it.

And, topping democracy, this most alluring record, that it alone can bind, and ever seeks to bind, all nations, all men, of however various and distant lands, into a brotherhood, a family. It is the old, yet ever-modern dream of earth, out of her eldest and her youngest, her fond philosophers and poets. Not that half only, individualism, which isolates. There is another half, which is adhesiveness or love, that fuses, ties and aggregates, making the races comrades, and fraternizing all. Both are to be vitalized by religion, (sole worthiest elevator of man or State,) breathing into the proud, material tissues, the breath of life. For I say at the core of democracy, finally, is the religious element. All the religions, old and new, are there. Nor may the scheme step forth, clothed in resplendent beauty and command, till these, bearing the best, the latest fruit, the spiritual, shall fully appear.

A portion of our pages we might indite with reference toward Europe, especially the British part of it, more than our own land, perhaps not absolutely needed for the home reader. But the whole question hangs together, and fastens and links all peoples. The liberalist of to-day has this advantage over antique or mediaeval times, that his doctrine seeks not only to individualize but to universalize. The great word Solidarity has arisen. Of all dangers to a nation, as things exist in our day, there can be no greater one than having certain portions of the people set off from the rest by a line drawn — they not privileged as others, but degraded, humiliated, made of no account. Much quackery teems, of course, even on democracy's side, yet does not really affect the orbic quality of the matter. To work in, if we may so term it, and justify God, his divine aggregate, the People, (or, the veritable horn'd and sharp-tail'd Devil, *his* aggregate, if there be who convulsively insist upon it) — this, I say, is what democracy is for; and this is what our America means and is doing — may I not say, has done? If not, she means nothing more, and does nothing more, than any other land. And as, by virtue of its kosmical, antiseptic power, Nature's stomach is fully strong enough not only to digest the morbific matter always presented, not to be turn'd aside, and perhaps, indeed, intuitively gravitating thither — but even to change such contributions into nutriment for highest use and life — so American democracy's. That is the lesson we, these days, send over to European lands by every western breeze.

And, truly, whatever may be said in the way of abstract argument, for or against the theory of a wider democratizing of institutions in any civilized country, much trouble might well be saved to all European lands by recognizing this palpable fact, (for a palpable fact it is,) that some form of such democratizing is about the only resource now left. *That,* or chronic dissatisfaction continued, mutterings which grow annually louder and louder, till, in due course, and pretty swiftly in most cases, the inevitable crisis, crash, dynastic ruin. Anything worthy to be call'd statesmanship in the Old World, I should say, among the advanced students, adepts, or men of any brains, does not debate to-day whether to hold on, attempting to lean back and monarchize, or to look forward and democratize — but *how*, and in what degree and part, most prudently to democratize.

The eager and often inconsiderate appeals of reformers and revolutionists are indispensable, to counterbalance the inertness and fossilism making so large a part of human institutions. The latter will always take care of themselves — the danger being that they rapidly tend to ossify us. The former is to be treated with indulgence, and even with respect. As circulation to air, so is agitation and a plentiful degree of speculative license to political and moral sanity. Indirectly, but surely, goodness, virtue, law, (of the very best,) follow freedom. These, to democracy, are what the keel is to the ship, or saltness to the ocean.

The true gravitation-hold of liberalism in the United States will be a more universal ownership of property, general homesteads, general comfort — a vast, intertwining reticulation of wealth. As the human frame, or, indeed, any object in this manifold universe, is best kept together by the simple miracle of its own cohesion, and the necessity, exercise and profit thereof, so a great and varied nationality, occupying millions of square miles, were firmest held and knit by the principle of the safety and endurance of the aggregate of its middling property owners. So that, from another point of view, ungracious as it may sound, and a paradox after what we have been saying, democracy looks with suspicious, ill-satisfied eye upon the very poor, the ignorant, and on those out of business. She asks for men and women with occupations, well-off, owners of houses and acres, and with cash in the bank — and with some cravings for literature, too; and must have them, and hastens to make

them. Luckily, the seed is already well-sown, and has taken ineradicable root.

Huge and mighty are our days, our republican lands — and most in their rapid shiftings, their changes, all in the interest of the cause. As I write this particular passage, (November, 1868,) the din of disputation rages around me. Acrid the temper of the parties, vital the pending questions. Congress convenes; the President sends his message; reconstruction is still in abeyance; the nomination and the contest for the twenty-first Presidentiad draw close, with loudest threat and bustle. Of these, and all the like of these, the eventuations I know not; but well I know that behind them, and whatever their eventuations, the vital things remain safe and certain, and all the needed work goes on. Time, with soon or later superciliousness, disposes of Presidents, Congressmen, party platforms, and such. Anon, it clears the stage of each and any mortal shred that thinks itself so potent to its day; and at and after which, (with precious, golden exceptions once or twice in a century,) all that relates to sir potency is flung to moulder in a burial-vault, and no one bothers himself the least bit about it afterward. But the People ever remain, tendencies continue, and all the idiocratic transfers in unbroken chain go on.

In a few years the dominion-heart of America will be far inland, toward the West. Our future national capitol may not be where the present one is. It is possible, nay likely, that in less than fifty years, it will migrate a thousand or two miles, will be re-founded, and every thing belonging to it made on a different plan, original, far more superb. The main social, political, spine-character of the States will probably run along the Ohio, Missouri and Mississippi rivers, and west and north of them, including Canada.

Those regions, with the group of powerful brothers toward the Pacific, (destined to the mastership of that sea and its countless paradises of islands,) will compact and settle the traits of America, with all the old retain'd, but more expanded, grafted on newer, hardier, purely native stock. A giant growth, composite from the rest, getting their contribution, absorbing it, to make it more illustrious. From the north, intellect, the sun of things, also the idea of unswayable justice, anchor amid the last, the wildest tempests. From the south the living soul, the animus of good and bad, haughtily admitting no demonstration but its own. While from the west itself comes solid personality, with blood and brawn, and the deep quality of all-accepting fusion.

Political democracy, as it exists and practically works in America, with all its threatening evils, supplies a training-school for making first-class men. It is life's gymnasium, not of good only, but of all. We try often, though we fall back often. A brave delight, fit for freedom's athletes, fills these arenas, and fully satisfies, out of the action in them, irrespective of success. Whatever we do not attain, we at any rate attain the experiences of the fight, the hardening of the strong campaign, and throb with currents of attempt at least. Time is ample. Let the victors come after us. Not for nothing does evil play its part among us. Judging from the main portions of the history of the world, so far, justice is always in jeopardy, peace walks amid hourly pitfalls, and of slavery, misery, meanness, the craft of tyrants and the credulity of the populace, in some of their protean forms, no voice can at any time say, They are not. The clouds break a little, and the sun shines out — but soon and certain the lowering darkness falls again, as if to last forever. Yet is there an immortal courage

and prophecy in every sane soul that cannot, must not, under any circumstances, capitulate. *Vive*, the attack — the perennial assault! *Vive*, the unpopular cause — the spirit that audaciously aims — the never-abandon'd efforts, pursued the same amid opposing proofs and precedents.

Once, before the war, (Alas! I dare not say how many times the mood has come!) I, too, was fill'd with doubt and gloom. A foreigner, an acute and good man, had impressively said to me, that day — putting in form, indeed, my own observations: "I have travel'd much in the United States, and watch'd their politicians, and listen'd to the speeches of the candidates, and read the journals, and gone into the public houses, and heard the unguarded talk of men. And I have found your vaunted America honeycomb'd from top to toe with infidelism, even to itself and its own programme. I have mark'd the brazen hell-faces of secession and slavery gazing defiantly from all the windows and doorways. I have everywhere found, primarily, thieves and scalliwags arranging the nominations to offices, and sometimes filling the offices themselves. I have found the north just as full of bad stuff as the south. Of the holders of public office in the Nation or the States or their municipalities, I have found that not one in a hundred has been chosen by any spontaneous selection of the outsiders, the people, but all have been nominated and put through by little or large caucuses of the politicians, and have got in by corrupt rings and electioneering, not capacity or desert. I have noticed how the millions of sturdy farmers and mechanics are thus the helpless supple-jacks of comparatively few politicians. And I have noticed more and more, the alarming spectacle of parties usurping the government, and openly and shamelessly wielding it for party purposes."

Sad, serious, deep truths. Yet are there other, still deeper, amply confronting, dominating truths. Over those politicians and great and little rings, and over all their insolence and wiles, and over the powerfulest parties, looms a power, too sluggish maybe, but ever holding decisions and decrees in hand, ready, with stern process, to execute them as soon as plainly needed — and at times, indeed, summarily crushing to atoms the mightiest parties, even in the hour of their pride.

In saner hours far different are the amounts of these things from what, at first sight, they appear. Though it is no doubt important who is elected governor, mayor, or legislator, (and full of dismay when incompetent or vile ones get elected, as they sometimes do,) there are other, quieter contingencies, infinitely more important. Shams, &c., will always be the show, like ocean's scum; enough, if waters deep and clear make up the rest. Enough, that while the piled embroider'd shoddy gaud and fraud spreads to the superficial eye, the hidden warp and weft are genuine, and will wear forever. Enough, in short, that the race, the land which could raise such as the late rebellion, could also put it down.

The average man of a land at last only is important. He, in these States, remains immortal owner and boss, deriving good uses, somehow, out of any sort of servant in office, even the basest; (certain universal requisites, and their settled regularity and protection, being first secured,) a nation like ours, in a sort of geological formation state, trying continually new experiments, choosing new delegations, is not served by the best men only, but sometimes more by those that provoke it — by the combats they arouse. Thus national rage, fury, discussion, &c.,

better than content. Thus, also, the warning signals, invaluable for after times.

What is more dramatic than the spectacle we have seen repeated, and doubtless long shall see — the popular judgment taking the successful candidates on trial in the offices — standing off, as it were, and observing them and their doings for a while, and always giving, finally, the fit, exactly due reward? I think, after all, the sublimest part of political history, and its culmination, is currently issuing from the American people. I know nothing grander, better exercise, better digestion, more positive proof of the past, the triumphant result of faith in human kind, than a well-contested American national election.

Then still the thought returns, (like the thread-passage in overtures,) giving the key and echo to these pages. When I pass to and fro, different latitudes, different seasons, beholding the crowds of the great cities, New York, Boston, Philadelphia, Cincinnati, Chicago, St. Louis, San Francisco, New Orleans, Baltimore — when I mix with these interminable swarms of alert, turbulent, good-natured, independent citizens, mechanics, clerks, young persons — at the idea of this mass of men, so fresh and free, so loving and so proud, a singular awe falls upon me. I feel, with dejection and amazement, that among our geniuses and talented writers or speakers, few or none have yet really spoken to this people, created a single image-making work for them, or absorb'd the central spirit and the idiosyncrasies which are theirs — and which, thus, in highest ranges, so far remain entirely uncelebrated, unexpress'd.

Dominion strong is the body's; dominion stronger is the mind's. What has fill'd, and fills to-day our intellect, our fancy, furnishing the standards therein, is yet foreign. The great poems, Shakespeare included, are poisonous to the idea of the pride and dignity of the common people, the lifeblood of democracy. The models of our literature, as we get it from other lands, ultramarine, have had their birth in courts, and bask'd and grown in castle sunshine; all smells of princes' favors. Of workers of a certain sort, we have, indeed, plenty, contributing after their kind; many elegant, many learn'd, all complacent. But touch'd by the national test, or tried by the standards of democratic personality, they wither to ashes. I say I have not seen a single writer, artist, lecturer, or what not, that has confronted the voiceless but ever erect and active, pervading, underlying will and typic aspiration of the land, in a spirit kindred to itself. Do you call those genteel little creatures American poets? Do you term that perpetual, pistareen, paste-pot work, American art, American drama, taste, verse? I think I hear, echoed as from some mountain-top afar in the west, the scornful laugh of the Genius of these States.

Democracy, in silence, biding its time, ponders its own ideals, not of literature and art only — not of men only, but of women. The idea of the women of America, (extricated from this daze, this fossil and unhealthy air which hangs about the word *lady*,) develop'd, raised to become the robust equals, workers, and, it may be, even practical and political deciders with the men — greater than man, we may admit, through their divine maternity, always their towering, emblematical attribute — but great, at any rate, as man, in all departments; or, rather, capable of being so, soon as they realize it, and can bring themselves to give up toys and fictions, and launch forth, as men do, amid real, independent, stormy life.

Then, as towards our thought's *finale*, (and, in that, over-arching the true scholar's lesson,) we have to say there can be no complete or epical presentation of democracy in the aggregate, or anything like it, at this day, because its doctrines will only be effectually incarnated in any one branch, when, in all, their spirit is at the root and centre. Far, far, indeed, stretch, in distance, our Vistas! How much is still to be disentangled, freed! How long it takes to make this American world see that it is, in itself, the final authority and reliance!

Did you, too, O friend, suppose democracy was only for elections, for politics, and for a party name? I say democracy is only of use there that it may pass on and come to its flower and fruits in manners, in the highest forms of interaction between men, and their beliefs — in religion, literature, colleges, and schools — democracy in all public and private life, and in the army and navy. I have intimated that, as a paramount scheme, it has yet few or no full realizers and believers. I do not see, either, that it owes any serious thanks to noted propagandists or champions, or has been essentially help'd, though often harm'd, by them. It has been and is carried on by all the moral forces, and by trade, finance, machinery, intercommunications, and, in fact, by all the developments of history, and can no more be stopp'd than the tides, or the earth in its orbit. Doubtless, also, it resides, crude and latent, well down in the hearts of the fair average of the American-born people, mainly in the agricultural regions. But it is not yet, there or anywhere, the fully-receiv'd, the fervid, the absolute faith.

I submit, therefore, that the fruition of democracy, on aught like a grand scale, resides altogether in the future. As, under any profound and comprehensive view of the gorgeous-composite feudal world, we see in it, through the long ages and cycles of ages, the results of a deep, integral, human and divine principle, or fountain, from which issued laws, ecclesia, manners, institutes, costumes, personalities, poems, (hitherto un-equall'd,) faithfully partaking of their source, and indeed only arising either to betoken it, or to furnish parts of that varied-flowing display, whose centre was one and absolute — so, long ages hence, shall the due historian or critic make at least an equal retrospect, an equal history for the democratic principle. It too must be adorn'd, credited with its results — then, when it, with imperial power, through amplest time, has dominated mankind — has been the source and test of all the moral, esthetic, social, political, and religious expressions and institutes of the civilized world — has begotten them in spirit and in form, and has carried them to its own unprecedented heights — has had, (it is possible,) monastics and ascetics, more numerous, more devout than the monks and priests of all previous creeds — has sway'd the ages with a breadth and rectitude tallying Nature's own — has fashion'd, systematized, and triumphantly finish'd and carried out, in its own interest, and with unparallel'd success, a new earth and a new man.

Vernon L. Parrington: THE AMERICAN SCENE

Changing America

When America laid aside its arms after Appomattox and turned back to the pursuits of peace it was well advanced toward the goal set by Alexander Hamilton three-quarters of a century before. The great obstacle that had withheld its feet hitherto had been swept from its path. A slave economy could never again thwart the ambitions of the capitalistic economy. The jealous particularism that for a generation had obstructed the inevitable drift toward a coalescing national unity had gone down in defeat. The agrarian South was no longer master in the councils of government; the shaping of the future had fallen to other hands and the unfolding of the new order could go forward without southern let or hindrance.

Other obstacles were falling away of themselves. North as well as South, the traditional domestic economy was already a thing of the past. An easier way to wealth, and one enormously more profitable, had been discovered. The future lay in the hands of the machine that was already dispossessing the tool. In the hurry of the war years the potentialities of the factory system had been explored and the ready resources of liquid capital had been greatly augmented. From the smoke of the great conflict an America had emerged unlike any the earlier generations had known. An ambitious industrialism stood on the threshold of a continental expansion that was to transfer sovereignty in America from a landed and mercantile aristocracy to the capable hands of a new race of captains of industry. Only the western farmers, newly settled in the Middle Border and spreading the psychology of the frontier through the vast prairie spaces of a greater Inland Empire, remained as a last stumbling-block. Other battles with agrarianism must be fought before capitalism assumed undisputed mastery of America; but with the eventual overthrow of the agrarian hosts in their last stronghold the path would lie broad and straight to the goal of an encompassing industrialism, with politicians and political parties its willing servants. There would be no more dissensions in the household. With southern Jeffersonians and western agrarians no longer sitting as watch dogs to the Constitution, the political state would be refashioned to serve a new age, and the old dream of a coalescing national economy become a reality. The American System was in the way of complete establishment.

Other changes impended, and greater. The enthronement of the machine was only the outward and visible sign of the revolution in thought that came with the rise of science. As a new cosmos unfolded before the inquisitive eyes of scientists the old metaphysical speculations became as obsolete as the old household economy. A new spirit of realism was abroad, probing and questioning the material world, pushing the realm of exact knowledge into the earlier regions of faith. The conquest of nature was the great business of the day, and as that conquest went forward triumphantly the solid fruits of the new mastery were gathered by industrialism. Science and the machine were the twin instruments for creating a new civilization, of which the technologist and the industrialist were the high priests. The transcendental theologian was soon to be as extinct as the passenger pigeon.

With the substitution of the captain of industry for the plantation master as the custodian of society, the age of aristocracy was at an end and the age of the middle class was established. A new culture, created by the machine and answering the needs of capitalism, was to dispossess the old culture with its lingering concern for distinction and its love of standards — a culture that should eventually suffice the needs of a brisk city world of machine activities. But that would take time. In the meanwhile — in the confused interregnum between reigns — America would be little more than a welter of crude energy, a raw unlovely society where the strife of competition with its prodigal waste testified to the shortcomings of an age in process of transition. The spirit of the frontier was to flare up in a huge buccaneering orgy. Having swept across the continent to the Pacific coast like a visitation of locusts, the frontier spirit turned back upon its course to conquer the East, infecting the new industrialism with a crude individualism, fouling the halls of Congress, despoiling the public domain, and indulging in a huge national barbecue. It submerged the arts and created a new literature. For a time it carried all things before it, until running full tilt into science and the machine, its triumphant progress was stopped and America, re-

jecting individualism, began the work of standardization and mechanization. It is this world in transition from an aristocratic to a middle-class order, turmoiled by the last flare-up of the frontier spirit, shifting from a robust individualism to a colorless standardization, which the chapters that follow must deal with. A confused and turbulent scene, but not without its fascination to the American who would understand his special heritage — perhaps the most characteristically native, the most American, in our total history.

Free America

The pot was boiling briskly in America in the tumultuous post-war years. The country had definitely entered upon its freedom and was settling its disordered household to suit its democratic taste. Everywhere new ways were feverishly at work transforming the countryside. In the South another order was rising uncertainly on the ruins of the plantation system; in the East an expanding factory economy was weaving a different pattern of industrial life; in the Middle Border a recrudescent agriculture was arising from the application of the machine to the rich prairie soil. All over the land a spider web of iron rails was being spun that was to draw the remotest outposts into the common whole and bind the nation together with steel bands. Nevertheless two diverse worlds lay on the map of continental America. Facing in opposite directions and holding different faiths, they would not travel together easily or take comfort from the yoke that joined them. Agricultural America, behind which lay two and a half centuries of experience, was a decentralized world, democratic, individualistic, suspicious; industrial America, behind which lay only half a dozen decades of bustling experiment, was a centralizing world, capitalistic, feudal, ambitious. The one was a decaying order, the other a rising, and between them would be friction till one or the other had become master.

Continental America was still half frontier and half settled country. A thin line of homesteads had been thrust westward till the outposts reached well into the Middle Border — an uncertain thread running through eastern Minnesota, Nebraska, Kansas, overleaping the Indian Territory and then running west into Texas — approximately halfway between the Atlantic and the Pacific. Behind these outposts was still much unoccupied land, and beyond stretched the unfenced prairies till they merged in the sagebrush plains, gray and waste, that stretched to the foothills of the Rocky Mountains. Beyond the mountains were other stretches of plains and deserts, vast and forbidding in their alkali blight, to the wooded coast ranges and the Pacific Ocean. In all this immense territory were only scattered settlements — at Denver, Salt Lake City, Sacramento, San Francisco, Portland, Seattle, and elsewhere — tiny outposts in the wilderness, with scattered hamlets, mining camps, and isolated homesteads lost in the great expanse. On the prairies from Mexico to Canada — across which rumbled great herds of buffalo — roved powerful tribes of hostile Indians who fretted against the forward thrust of settlement and disputed the right of possession. The urgent business of the times was the subduing of this wild region, wresting it from Indians and buffalo and wilderness; and the forty years that lay between the California Gold Rush of '49 and the Oklahoma Land Rush of '89 saw the greatest wave of pioneer expansion — the swiftest and most reckless — in all our pioneer experience. Expansion on so vast a scale necessitated

building, and the seventies became the railway age, bonding the future to break down present barriers of isolation, and opening new territories for later exploitation. The reflux of the great movement swept back upon the Atlantic coast and gave to life there a fresh note of spontaneous vigor, of which the Gilded Age was the inevitable expression.

It was this energetic East, with its accumulations of liquid capital awaiting investment and its factories turning out the materials needed to push the settlements westward, that profited most from the conquest of the far West. The impulsion from the frontier did much to drive forward the industrial revolution. The war that brought devastation to the South had been more friendly to northern interests. In gathering the scattered rills of capital into central reservoirs at Philadelphia and New York, and in expanding the factory system to supply the needs of the armies, it had opened to capitalism its first clear view of the Promised Land. The bankers had come into control of the liquid wealth of the nation, and the industrialists had learned to use the machine for production; the time was ripe for exploitation on a scale undreamed-of a generation before. Up till then the potential resources of the continent had not even been surveyed. Earlier pioneers had only scratched the surface — felling trees, making crops, building pygmy watermills, smelting a little iron. Mineral wealth had been scarcely touched. Tools had been lacking to develop it, capital had been lacking, transportation lacking, technical methods lacking, markets lacking.

In the years following the war, exploitation for the first time was provided with adequate resources and a competent technique, and busy prospectors were daily uncovering new sources of wealth.

The coal and oil of Pennsylvania and Ohio, the copper and iron ore of upper Michigan, the gold and silver, lumber and fisheries, of the Pacific Coast, provided limitless raw materials for the rising industrialism. The Bessemer process quickly turned an age of iron into an age of steel and created the great rolling mills of Pittsburgh from which issued the rails for expanding railways. The reaper and binder, the sulky plow and the threshing machine, created a large-scale agriculture on the fertile prairies. Wild grass-lands provided grazing for immense herds of cattle and sheep; the development of the corn-belt enormously increased the supply of hogs; and with railways at hand the Middle Border poured into Omaha and Kansas City and Chicago an endless stream of produce. As the line of the frontier pushed westward new towns were built, thousands of homesteads were filed on, and the speculator and promoter hovered over the prairies like buzzards seeking their carrion. With rising land-values money was to be made out of un-earned increment, and the creation of booms was a profitable industry. The times were stirring and it was a shiftless fellow who did not make his pile. If he had been too late to file on desirable acres he had only to find a careless home-steader who had failed in some legal technicality and "jump his claim." Good bottom land could be had even by late-comers if they were sharp at the game.

This bustling America of 1870 accounted itself a democratic world. A free people had put away all aristocratic privileges and conscious of its power went forth to possess the last frontier. Its social philosophy, which it found adequate to its needs, was summed up in three words — preëmption, exploitation, progress. Its immediate and pressing business was to dispossess the government of its rich holdings. Lands in the possession of the government were so much idle waste, untaxed and profitless; in private hands they would be developed. They would provide work, pay taxes, support schools, enrich the community. Preëmption meant exploitation and exploitation meant progress. It was a simple philosophy and it suited the simple individualism of the times. The Gilded Age knew nothing of the Enlightenment; it recognized only the acquisitive instinct. That much at least the frontier had taught the great American democracy; and in applying to the resources of a continent the lesson it had been so well taught the Gilded Age wrote a profoundly characteristic chapter of American history.

Figures of Earth

In a moment of special irritation Edwin Lawrence Godkin called the civilization of the seventies a chromo civilization. Mark Twain, with his slack western standards, was equally severe. As he contemplated the slovenly reality beneath the gaudy exterior he dubbed it the Gilded Age. Other critics with a gift for pungent phrase have flung their gibes at the ways of a picturesque and uncouth generation. There is reason in plenty for such caustic comment. Heedless, irreverent, unlovely, cultivating huge beards, shod in polished top-boots — the last refinement of the farmer's cowhides — wearing linen dickeys over hickory shirts, moving through pools of tobacco juice, erupting in shoddy and grotesque architecture, cluttering its homes with ungainly walnut chairs and marble-topped tables and heavy lambrequins, the decade of the seventies was only too plainly mired and floundering in a bog of bad taste. A world of triumphant and unabashed vulgarity without its like in our history, it was not aware of its plight, but accounted its manners genteel and boasted of ways that were a parody on sober good sense.

Yet just as such comments are, they do not reach quite to the heart of the age. They emphasize rather the excrescences, the casual lapses, of a generation that underneath its crudities and vulgarities was boldly adventurous and creative — a generation in which the democratic freedoms of America, as those freedoms had taken shape during a drab frontier experience, came at last to spontaneous and vivid expression. If its cultural wealth was less than it thought, if in its exuberance it was engaged somewhat too boisterously in stamping its own plebeian image on the work of its hands, it was only natural to a society that for the first time found its opportunities equal to its desires, a youthful society that accounted the world its oyster and wanted no restrictions laid on its will. It was the ripe fruit of Jacksonian leveling, and if it ran to a grotesque individualism — if in its self-confidence it was heedless of the smiles of older societies — it was nevertheless by reason of its uncouthness the most picturesque generation in our history; and for those who love to watch human nature disporting itself with naïve abandon, running amuck through all the conventions, no other age provides so fascinating a spectacle.

When the cannon at last had ceased their destruction it was a strange new America that looked out confidently on the scene. Something had been released by the upheavals of half a century, something strong and assertive that was prepared to take possession of the continent. It did not issue from the loins of war. Its origins must be sought elsewhere, further back in time. It had been cradled in the vast changes that since 1815 had been re-shaping America: in the break-up of the old domestic economy that kept life mean and drab, in the noisy enthusiasms of the new coonskin democracy, in the romanticisms of the California gold rush, in the boisterous freedoms discovered by the forties and fifties. It had come to manhood in the battles of a tremendous war, and as it now surveyed the continent, discovering potential wealth before unknown, it demanded only freedom and opportunity — a fair race and no favors. Everywhere was a welling-up of primitive pagan desires after long repressions — to grow rich, to grasp power, to be strong and masterful and lay the world at its feet. It was a violent reaction from the narrow poverty of frontier life and the narrow inhibitions of backwoods religion. It had had enough of skimpy, meager ways, of scrubbing along hoping for something to turn up. It would go out and turn it up. It was consumed with a great hunger for abundance, for the good things of life, for wealth. It was frankly materialistic and if material goods could be wrested from society it would lay its hands heartily to the work. Freedom and opportunity, to acquire, to possess, to enjoy — for that it would sell its soul.

Society of a sudden was become fluid. With the sweeping-away of the last aristocratic restraints the potentialities of the common man found release for self-assertion. Strange figures, sprung from obscure origins, thrust themselves everywhere upon the scene. In the reaction from the mean and skimpy, a passionate will to power was issuing from unexpected sources, undisciplined, confused in ethical values, but endowed with immense vitality. Individualism was being simplified to the acquisitive instinct. These new Americans were primitive souls, ruthless, predatory, capable; single-minded men; rogues and rascals often, but never feeble, never hindered by petty scruple, never given to puling or whining — the raw materials of a race of capitalistic buccaneers. Out of the drab mass of common plebeian life had come this vital energy that erupted in amazing abundance and in strange forms. The new freedoms meant diverse things to different men and each like Jurgen followed after his own wishes and his own desires. Pirate and priest issued from the common source and played their parts with the same picturesqueness. The romantic age of Captain Kidd was come again, and the black flag and the gospel banner were both in lockers to be flown as the needs of the cruise determined. With all coercive restrictions put away the democratic genius of America was setting out on the road of manifest destiny.

Analyze the most talked-of men of the age and one is likely to find a splendid audacity coupled with an immense wastefulness. A note of tough-mindedness marks them. They had stout nippers. They fought their way encased in rhinoceros hides. There was the Wall Street crowd — Daniel Drew, Commodore Vanderbilt, Jim Fisk, Jay Gould, Russell Sage — blackguards for the most part, railway wreckers, cheaters and swindlers, but picturesque in their rascality. There was the numerous tribe of politicians — Boss Tweed, Fernando Wood, G. Oakey Hall, Senator Pomeroy, Senator Cameron, Roscoe Conkling, James G. Blaine — blackguards also for the most part, looting city treasuries, buying and selling legislative votes like railway stock, but picturesque in their audacity. There were the professional keepers of the public morals — Anthony Comstock, John B. Gough, Dwight L. Moody, Henry Ward Beecher, T. De Witt Talmage — ardent proselytizers, unintellectual, men of one

idea, but fiery in zeal and eloquent in description of the particular heaven each wanted to people with his fellow Americans. And springing up like mushrooms after a rain was the goodly company of cranks — Victoria Woodhull and Tennessee Claflin, "Citizen" George Francis Train, Henry Bergh, Ben Butler, Ignatius Donnelly, Bob Ingersoll, Henry George — picturesque figures with a flair for publicity who tilled their special fields with splendid gestures. And finally there was Barnum the Showman, growing rich on the profession of humbuggery, a vulgar greasy genius, pure brass without any gilding, yet in picturesque and capable effrontery the very embodiment of the age. A marvelous company, vital with the untamed energy of a new land. In the presence of such men one begins to understand what Walt Whitman meant by his talk of the elemental.

Created by a primitive world that knew not the machine, they were marked by the rough homeliness of their origins. Whether wizened or fat they were never insignificant or commonplace. On the whole one prefers them fat, and for solid bulk what generation has outdone them? There was Revivalist Moody, bearded and neckless, with his two hundred and eighty pounds of Adam's flesh, every ounce of which "belonged to God." There was the lyric Sankey, afflicted with two hundred and twenty-five pounds of human frailty, yet looking as smug as a banker and singing "There were ninety and nine" divinely through mutton-chop whiskers. There was Boss Tweed, phlegmatic and mighty, overawing rebellious gangsters at the City Hall with his two hundred and forty pounds of pugnacious rascality. There was John Fiske, a philosophic hippopotamus, warming the chill waters of Spencerian science with his prodigious bulk. There was Ben Butler, oily and puffy and wheezy, like Falstaff larding the lean earth as he walked along, who yearly added more flesh to the scant ninety-seven pounds he carried away from Waterville College. And there was Jim Fisk, dressed like a bartender, huge in nerve as in bulk, driving with the dashing Josie Mansfield down Broadway — prince of vulgarians, who jovially proclaimed, "I worship in the Synagogue of the Libertines," and who on the failure of the Erie coup announced cheerfully, "Nothing is lost save honor!"

Impressive as are the fat kine of Egypt, the lean kine scarcely suffer by contrast. There were giants of puny physique in those days. There was Uncle Dan'l Drew, thin as a dried herring, yet a builder of churches and founder of Drew Theological Seminary, who pilfered and cheated his way to wealth with tobacco juice drooling from his mouth. There was Jay Gould, a lone-hand gambler, a dynamo in a tubercular body, who openly invested in the devil's tenements as likely to pay better dividends, and went home to potter lovingly amongst his exotic flowers. And there was Oakey Hall, clubman and playwright, small, elegant, and unscrupulous; and Victoria Woodhull who stirred up the Beecher case, a wisp of a woman who enraged all the frumpy blue-stockings by the smartness of her toilet and the perfection of her manners; and little Libby Tilton with her tiny wistful face and great eyes that looked out wonderingly at the world — eyes that were to go blind with weeping before the candle of her life went out. It was such men and women, individual and colorful, that Whitman and Mark Twain mingled with, and that Herman Melville — colossal and dynamic beyond them all — looked out upon sardonically from his tomb in the Custom House where he was consuming his own heart.

They were thrown up as it were casually out of the huge caldron of energy that was America. All over the land were thousands like them, self-made men quick to lay hands on opportunity if it knocked at the door, ready to seek it out if it were slow in knocking, recognizing no limitations to their powers, discouraged by no shortcomings in their training. When Moody set out to bring the world to his Protestant God he was an illiterate shoe salesman who stumbled over the hard words of his King James Bible. Anthony Comstock, the roundsman of the Lord, was a salesman in a dry-goods shop, and as careless of his spelling as he was careful of his neighbors' morals. Commodore Vanderbilt, who built up the greatest fortune of the time, was a Brooklyn ferryman, hardfisted and tough as a burr-oak, who in a lifetime of over eighty years read only one book, *Pilgrim's Progress,* and that after he was seventy. Daniel Drew was a shyster cattle-drover, whose arid emotions found outlet in periodic conversions and backslidings, and who got on in this vale of tears by salting his cattle and increasing his — and the Lord's — wealth with every pound of water in their bellies — from which cleverness is said to have come the Wall Street phrase, "stock-watering." Jim Fisk was the son of a Yankee peddler, who, disdaining the unambitious ways of his father, set up for himself in a cart gilded like a circus-wagon and drove about the countryside with jingling bells. After he had made his pile in Wall Street he set up his own opera house and proposed to rival the Medici as a patron of the arts — and especially of the artists if they were of the right sex. A surprising number of them — Moody, Beecher, Barnum, Fisk, Comstock, Ben Butler — came from New England; Jay Gould was of Connecticut ancestry; but Oakey Hall was a southern gentleman; Fernando Wood, with the face of an Apollo and the wit of an Irishman, was the son of a Philadelphia cigarmaker and much of his early income was drawn from sailors' groggeries along the waterfront; Tweed was a stolid New Yorker, and Drew was a York State country boy.

What was happening in New York was symptomatic of the nation. If the temple of Plutus was building in Wall Street, his devotees were everywhere. In Chicago, rising higgledy-piggledy from the ashes of the great fire, Phil Armour and Nelson Morris were laying out stockyards and drawing the cattle and sheep and hogs from remote prairie farms to their slaughter-houses. In Cleveland, Mark Hanna was erecting his smelters and turning the iron ore of Michigan into dollars, while John D. Rockefeller was squeezing the small fry out of the petroleum business and creating the Standard Oil monopoly. In Pittsburgh, Andrew Carnegie was applying the Bessemer process to steel-making and laying the foundations of the later steel trust. In Minneapolis, C. C. Washburn and Charles A. Pillsbury were applying new methods to milling and turning the northern wheat into flour to ship to the ends of the earth. In San Francisco, Leland Stanford and Collis P. Huntington were amassing huge fortunes out of the Southern Pacific Railway and bringing the commonwealth of California to their feet. Everywhere were boom-town and real-estate promoters, the lust of speculation, the hankering after quick and easy wealth.

In the great spaces from Kansas City to Sacramento the frontier spirit was in the gaudiest bloom. The experiences of three centuries of expansion were being crowded into as many decades. In the fifties the highway of the frontier had run up and down the Mississippi River and the golden age of steamboating had brought a motley life to Saint Louis; in the seventies the frontier had passed far beyond and was pushing through the Rocky Mountains, repeating as it went the old frontier story of swagger and slovenliness, of boundless hope and heroic endurance — a story deeply marked with violence and crime and heartbreaking failure. Thousands of veterans from the disbanded armies, northern and southern alike, flocked to the West to seek their fortunes, and daily life there soon took on a drab note from the alkali of the plains; yet through the drabness ran a boisterous humor that exalted lying to a fine art — a humor that goes back to Davy Crockett and the Ohio flatboatmen. Mark Twain's *Roughing It* is the epic of this frontier of the Pony Express, as *Life on the Mississippi* is the epic of the preceding generation.

The huge wastefulness of the frontier was everywhere, East and West. The Gilded Age heeded somewhat too literally the Biblical injunction to take no thought for the morrow, but was busily intent on squandering the resources of the continent. All things were held cheap, and human life cheapest of all. Wild Bill Hickok with forty notches on his gun and a row of graves to his credit in Boot Hill Cemetery, and Jesse James, most picturesque of desperadoes, levying toll with his six-shooter on the bankers who were desecrating the free spirit of the plains with their two per cent. a month, are familiar heroes in Wild West tales; but the real plainsman of the Gilded Age, the picturesque embodiment of the last frontier, was Captain Carver, the faultless horseman and faultless shot, engaged in his celebrated buffalo hunt for the championship of the prairies. Wagering that he could kill more buffalo in a day than any rival hero of the chase, he rode forth with his Indian marker and dropping the miles behind him he left an endless trail of dead beasts properly tagged, winning handsomely when his rival's horse fell dead from exhaustion. It was magnificent. Davy Crockett's hundred and five bears in a season was but 'prentice work compared with Captain Carver's professional skill. It is small wonder that he became a hero of the day and his rifle, turned now to the circus business of breaking glass balls thrown from his running horse, achieved a fame far greater than Davy's Betsy. With his bold mustaches, his long black hair flying in the wind, his sombrero and chaps and top-boots, he was a figure matched only by Buffalo Bill, the last of the great plainsmen.

Captain Carver was picturesque, but what shall be said of the thousands of lesser Carvers engaged in the same slaughter, market-hunters who discovered a new industry in buffalo-killing? At the close of the Civil War the number on the western plains was estimated at fifteen millions. With the building of the Union Pacific Railroad they were cut asunder into two vast herds, and upon these herds fell the hunters with the new breech-loading rifles, shooting for the hide market that paid sixty-five cents for a bull's hide and a dollar and fifteen cents for a cow's. During the four years from 1871 to 1874 nearly a million head a year were slain from the southern herd alone, their skins ripped off and the carcasses left for the coyotes and buzzards. By the end of the hunting-season of 1875 the vast southern herd had been wiped out, and with the building of the North-ern Pacific in 1880 the smaller northern herd soon suffered the same fate. The buffalo were gone with the hostile Indians — Sioux and Blackfeet and Cheyennes and a dozen other tribes.[1] It was the last dramatic episode of the American frontier, and it wrote a fitting climax to three centuries of wasteful conquest. But the prairies were tamed, and Wild Bill Hickok and Captain Carver and Buffalo Bill Cody had become romantic figures to enthrall the imagination of later generations.[2]

It was an abundant harvest of those freedoms that America had long been struggling to achieve, and it was making ready the ground for later harvests that would be less to its liking. Freedom had become individualism, and individualism had become the inalienable right to preempt, to exploit, to squander. Gone were the old ideals along with the old restraints. The idealism of the forties, the romanticism of the fifties — all the heritage of Jeffersonianism and the French Enlightenment — were put thoughtlessly away, and with no social conscience, no concern for civilization, no heed for the future of the democracy it talked so much about, the Gilded Age threw itself into the business of money-getting. From the sober restraints of aristocracy, the old inhibitions of Puritanism, the niggardliness of an exacting domestic economy, it

[1] See Allan Nevins, "The Taming of the West," in *The Emergence of Modern America.*

[2] It is the same story in the matter of the passenger pigeon. In early days the flights of these birds ran to untold millions. The last great nesting was at Petoskey, Michigan, in 1878, covering a strip forty miles long and from three to ten miles wide. Upon the nests fell the market-hunters and a million and a half squabs were shipped to New York by rail, besides the thousands wasted. Within a generation the passenger pigeon had become extinct. See W. B. Mershon, *Outdoor Life and Recreation*, February, 1929, p. 26 ff.

swung far back in reaction, and with the discovery of limitless opportunities for exploitation it allowed itself to get drunk. Figures of earth, they followed after their own dreams. Some were builders with grandiose plans in their pockets; others were wreckers with no plans at all. It was an anarchistic world of strong, capable men, selfish, unenlightened, amoral — an excellent example of what human nature will do with undisciplined freedom. In the Gilded Age freedom was the freedom of buccaneers preying on the argosies of Spain.

Politics and the Fairy Godmother

Certainly the Gilded Age would have resented such an interpretation of its brisk activities. In the welter of change that resulted from the application of the machine to the raw materials of a continent, it chose rather to see the spirit of progress to which the temper of the American people was so responsive. Freedom, it was convinced, was justifying itself by its works. The eighteenth century had been static, the nineteenth century was progressive. It was adaptable, quick to change its ways and its tools, ready to accept whatever proved advantageous — pragmatic, opportunist. It was not stifled by the dead hand of custom but was free to adapt means to ends. It accepted progress as it accepted democracy, without questioning the sufficiency of either. The conception accorded naturally with a frontier psychology. Complete opportunism is possible only amongst a people that is shallow-rooted, that lives in a fluid society, scantily institutionalized, with few vested interests. In a young society it is easy, in a maturing society it becomes increasingly difficult.

Dazzled by the results of the new technique of exploitation applied on a grand scale to unpreëmpted opportunities, it is no wonder the Gilded Age thought well of its labors and confused the pattern of life it was weaving with the pattern of a rational civilization. It had drunk in the idea of progress with its mother's milk. It was an inevitable frontier interpretation of the swift changes resulting from a fluid economics and a fluid society in process of settling into static ways. It served conveniently to describe the changes from the simplicities of social beginnings to the complexities of a later order. It was made use of following the War of 1812 to explain the stir resulting from the westward expansion and the great increase in immigration; but it was given vastly greater significance by the social unsettlements that came with the industrial revolution. With the realization of the dramatic changes in manner of living — the added conveniences of life, release from the laborious round of the domestic economy, ease of transportation — that resulted from the machine order, it was inevitable that the idea of progress should have been on every man's tongue. The increase of wealth visible to all was in itself a sufficient sign of progress, and as the novelty of the industrial change wore off and the economy of America was more completely industrialized, it was this augmenting wealth that symbolized it.

In such fashion the excellent ideal of progress that issued from the social enthusiasms of the Enlightenment was taken in charge by the Gilded Age and transformed into a handmaid of capitalism. Its duties were narrowed to the single end of serving profits and its accomplishments came to be exactly measured by bank clearings. It was unfortunate but inevitable. The idea was too seductive to the American mentality not to be seized upon and made to serve a rising order. Exploitation was the business of the times and how better could exploitation throw about its activities the sanction of idealism than by wedding them to progress? It is a misfortune that America has never subjected the abstract idea of progress to critical examination. Content with the frontier and capitalistic interpretations it has confused change with betterment, and when a great idealist of the Gilded Age demonstrated to America that it was misled and pointed out that the path of progress it was following was the highway to poverty, he was hooted from the market-place.

Having thus thrown the mantle of progress about the Gold Dust twins, the Gilded Age was ready to bring the political forces of America into harmony with the program of preëmption and exploitation. The situation could hardly have been more to its liking. Post-war America was wholly lacking in political philosophies, wholly opportunist. The old party cleavage between agriculture and industry had been obscured and the logic of party alignment destroyed by the struggle over slavery. Democrat and Whig no longer faced each other conscious of the different ends they sought. The great party of Jefferson and Jackson was prostrate, borne down by the odium of slavery and secession. In the North elements of both had been drawn into a motley war party, momentarily fused by the bitterness of conflict, but lacking any common program, certain indeed to split on fundamental economic issues. The Whig Republican was still Hamiltonian paternalistic, and the Democrat Republican was still Jeffersonian *laissez faire,* and until it was determined which wing should control the party councils there would be only confusion. The politicians were fertile in compromises, but in nominating Lincoln and Johnson the party ventured to get astride two horses that would not run together. To attempt to make yoke-fellows of democratic leveling and capitalistic paternalism was prophetic of rifts and schisms that only the passions of Reconstruction days could hold in check.

In 1865 the Republican party was no other than a war machine that had accomplished its purpose. It was a political mongrel, without logical cohesion, and it seemed doomed to break up as the Whig party had broken up and the Federalist party had broken up. But fate was now on the side of the Whigs as it had not been earlier. The democratic forces had lost strength from the war, and democratic principles were in ill repute. The drift to centralization, the enormous development of capitalism, the spirit of exploitation, were prophetic of a changing temper that was preparing to exalt the doctrine of manifest destiny which the Whig party stood sponsor for. The middle class was in the saddle and it was time to bring the political state under its control. The practical problem of the moment was to transform the mongrel Republican party into a strong cohesive instrument, and to accomplish that it was necessary to hold the loyalty of its Democratic voters amongst the farmers and working-classes whilst putting into effect its Whig program.

Under normal conditions the thing would have been impossible, but the times were wrought up and blindly passionate and the politicians skillful. The revolt of Andrew Johnson came near to bringing the party on the rocks; but the undisciplined Jacksonians were overthrown by the appeal to the Bloody Flag and put to flight by the nomination of General Grant for the presidency. The rebellion of the Independent Republicans under Horace Greeley in 1872 was brought to nothing by the skillful use of Grant's military prestige, and the party passed definitely under the control of capitalism, and became such an instrument for exploitation as Henry Clay dreamed of but could not perfect. Under the nominal leadership of the easy-going Grant a loose rein was given to Whiggish ambitions and the Republican party became a political instrument worthy of the Gilded Age.

The triumph of Whiggery was possible because the spirit of the Gilded Age was Whiggish. The picturesque embodiment of the multitude of voters who hurrahed for Grant and the Grand Old Party was a figure who had grown his first beard in the ebullient days before Secession. Colonel Beriah Sellers, with his genial optimism and easy political ethics, was an epitome of the political hopes of the Gilded Age. With a Micawber-like faith in his country and his government, eager to realize on his expansive dreams and looking to the national treasury to scatter its fructifying millions in the neighborhood of his speculative holdings, he was no other than Uncle Sam in the boisterous days following Appomattox. The hopes that floated up out of his dreams were the hopes of millions who cast their votes for Republican Congressmen who in return were expected to cast their votes for huge governmental appropriations that would insure prosperity's reaching certain post-office addresses. Citizens had saved the government in the trying days that were past; it was only fair in return that government should aid the patriotic citizen in the necessary work of developing national resources. It was paternalism as understood by speculators and subsidy-hunters, but was it not a part of the great American System that was to make the country rich and self-sufficient?

The American System had been talked of for forty years; it had slowly got on its feet in pre-war days despite the stubborn planter opposition; now at last it had fairly come into its own. The time was ripe for the Republican party to become a fairy godmother to the millions of Beriah Sellerses throughout the North and West.

It is plain as a pikestaff why the spirit of Whiggery should have taken riotous possession of the Gilded Age. With its booming industrial cities America in 1870 was fast becoming capitalistic, and in every capitalistic society Whiggery springs up as naturally as pigweed in a garden. However attractive the disguises it may assume, it is in essence the logical creed of the profit philosophy. It is the expression in politics of the acquisitive instinct and it assumes as the greatest good the shaping of public policy to promote private interests. It asserts that it is a duty of the state to help its citizens to make money, and it conceives of the political state as a useful instrument for effective exploitation. How otherwise? The public good cannot be served apart from business interests, for business interests are the public good and in serving business the state is serving society. Everybody's eggs are in the basket and they must not be broken. For a capitalistic society Whiggery is the only rational politics, for it exalts the profit-motive as the sole object of parliamentary concern. Government has only to wave its wand and fairy gifts descend upon business like the golden sands of Pactolus. It graciously bestows its tariffs and subsidies, and streams of wealth flow into private wells.

But unhappily there is a fly in the Whiggish honey. In a competitive order, government is forced to make its choices. It cannot serve both Peter and Paul. If it gives with one hand it must take away with the other. And so the persuasive ideal of paternalism in the common interest degenerates in practice into legalized favoritism. Governmental gifts go to the largest investments. Lesser interests are sacrificed to greater interests and Whiggery comes finally to serve the lords of the earth without whose good will the wheels of business will not turn. To him that hath shall be given. If the few do not prosper the many will starve, and if the many have bread who would begrudge the few their abundance? In Whiggery is the fulfillment of the Scriptures.

Henry Clay had been a prophetic figure pointing the way America was to travel; but he came a generation too soon. A son of the Gilded Age, he was doomed to live in a world of Jacksonian democracy. But the spirit of Henry Clay survived his death and his followers were everywhere in the land. The plain citizen who wanted a slice of the rich prairie land of Iowa or Kansas, with a railway convenient to his homestead, had learned to look to the government for a gift, and if he got his quarter-section and his transportation he was careless about what the other fellow got. A little more or less could make no difference to a country inexhaustible in resources. America belonged to the American people and not to the government, and resources in private hands paid taxes and increased the national wealth. In his favorite newspaper, the *New York Tribune,* he read daily appeals for the adoption of a patriotic national economy, by means of which an infant industrialism, made prosperous by a protective tariff, would provide a home market for the produce of the farmer and render the country self-sufficient. Money would thus be put in everybody's pocket. Protection was not

robbing Peter to pay Paul, but paying both Peter and Paul out of the augmented wealth of the whole.

The seductive arguments that Horace Greeley disseminated amongst the plain people, Henry Carey purveyed to more intelligent ears. The most distinguished American economist of the time, Carey had abandoned his earlier *laissez-faire* position, and having convinced himself that only through a close-knit national economy could the country develop a well-rounded economic program, he had become the most ardent of protectionists. During the fifties and later he was tireless in popularizing the doctrine of a natural harmony of interests between agriculture and manufacturing, and to a generation expanding rapidly in both fields his able presentation made great appeal. It was but a step from protectionism to governmental subsidies. Beriah Sellers and Henry Clay had come to be justified by the political economists. (Note that amongst Carey's converts were such different idealists as Wendell Phillips and Peter Cooper.)

The Great Barbecue

Horace Greeley and Henry Carey were only straws in the wind that during the Gilded Age was blowing the doctrine of paternalism about the land. A Colonel Sellers was to be found at every fireside talking the same blowsy doctrine. Infectious in their optimism, naïve in their faith that something would be turned up for them by the government if they made known their wants, they were hoping for dollars to be put in their pockets by a generous administration at Washington. Congress had rich gifts to bestow — in lands, tariffs, subsidies, favors of all sorts; and when influential citizens made their wishes known to the reigning statesmen, the sympathetic politicians were quick to turn the government into the fairy godmother the voters wanted it to be. A huge barbecue was spread to which all presumably were invited. Not quite all, to be sure; inconspicuous persons, those who were at home on the farm or at work in the mills and offices, were overlooked; a good many indeed out of the total number of the American people. But all the important persons, leading bankers and promoters and business men, received invitations. There wasn't room for everybody and these were presumed to represent the whole. It was a splendid feast. If the waiters saw to it that the choicest portions were served to favored guests, they were not unmindful of their numerous homespun constituency and they loudly proclaimed the fine democratic principle that what belongs to the people should be enjoyed by the people — not with petty bureaucratic restrictions, not as a social body, but as individuals, each free citizen using what came to hand for his own private ends, with no questions asked.

It was sound Gilded Age doctrine. To a frontier people what was more democratic than a barbecue, and to a paternalistic age what was more fitting than that the state should provide the beeves for roasting. Let all come and help themselves. As a result the feast was Gargantuan in its rough plenty. The abundance was what was to be expected of a generous people. More food, to be sure, was spoiled than was eaten, and the revelry was a bit unseemly; but it was a fine spree in the name of the people, and the invitations had been written years before by Henry Clay. But unfortunately what was intended to be jovially democratic was marred by displays of plebeian temper. Suspicious commoners with

better eyes than manners discovered the favoritism of the waiters and drew attention to the difference between their own meager helpings and the heaped-up plates of more favored guests. It appeared indeed that there was gross discrimination in the service; that the farmers' pickings from the Homestead Act were scanty in comparison with the speculators' pickings from the railway land-grants. The *Crédit Mobilier* scandal and the Whisky Ring scandal and divers other scandals came near to breaking up the feast, and the genial host — who was no other than the hero of Appomattox — came in for some sharp criticism. But after the more careless ones who were caught with their fingers where they didn't belong, had been thrust from the table, the eating and drinking went on again till only the great carcasses were left. Then at last came the reckoning. When the bill was sent in to the American people the farmers discovered that they had been put off with the giblets while the capitalists were consuming the turkey. They learned that they were no match at a barbecue for more voracious guests, and as they went home unsatisfied, a sullen anger burned in their hearts that was to express itself later in fierce agrarian revolts.

What reason there was for such anger, how differently rich and poor fared at the democratic feast, is suggested by the contrast between the Homestead Act and the Union Pacific land-grant. Both were war-time measures and both had emerged from the agitations of earlier decades. By the terms of the former the homesteader got his hundred and sixty acres at the price of $1.25 an acre; by the terms of the latter the promoters got a vast empire for nothing. It was absurd, of course, but what would you have? The people wanted the railway built and Collis P. Huntington was willing to build it on his own terms. The government was too generous to haggle with public-spirited citizens, and too Whiggish to want to discourage individual enterprise. Ever since the cession of California there had been much talk of a continental railway to tie the country together. In the first years the talk in Congress had all been of a great national venture; the road must be built by the nation to serve the common interests of the American people. But unfortunately sectional jealousies prevented any agreement as to the route the survey lines were to run, and the rising capitalism was becoming powerful enough to bring into disfavor any engagement of the government in a work that promised great rewards. Under its guidance political opinion was skillfully turned into the channel of private enterprise. The public domain backed by the public credit, it was agreed, must pay for the road, but the government must not seek to control the enterprise or look to profit from it directly; the national reward would come indirectly from the opening-up of vast new territories.

The definite shift in policy came about the year 1855. In 1837 Stephen A. Douglas had been the driving force behind the state enterprise of building the Illinois Central Railway. In 1853 he proposed that the Pacific Railroad should be built by private enterprise. With the change promptly came a request for a patriotic land-grant. The government was expected to provide the road, it appeared, but private enterprise was to own it and manage it in the interest of speculators rather than the public. For old-fashioned souls like Thomas H. Benton, who still remembered the Jeffersonian concern for

the common well-being, it was a bitter mess to swallow.

> I would have preferred [he said] that Congress should have made the road, as a national work, on a scale commensurate with its grandeur and let out the use of it to companies, who would fetch and carry on the best terms for the people and the government. But that hope has vanished . . . a private company has become the resource and the preference. I embrace it as such, utterly scouting all plans for making private roads at national expense, of paying for the use of roads built with our land and money, of bargaining with corporations or individuals for the use of what we give them.[3]

With this speech the old Jeffersonianism pulled down its flag and the new Whiggery ran up its black banner. The Gilded Age had begun and Old Bullion Benton had outlived his time. In the tumultuous decades that followed there was to be no bargaining with corporations for the use of what the public gave; they took what they wanted and no impertinent questions were asked. The hungriest will get the most at the barbecue. A careless wastefulness when the supply is unlimited is perhaps natural enough. There were hard-headed men in the world of Beriah Sellers who knew how easy it was to overreach the simple, and it was they who got most from the common pot. We may call them buccaneers if we choose, and speak of the great barbecue as a democratic debauch. But why single out a few, when all were drunk? Whisky was plentiful at barbecues, and if too liberal potations brought the Gilded Age to the grossest extravagancies, if when it cast up accounts it found its patrimony gone, it was only

3 Quoted in J. P. Davis, *The Union Pacific Railway*, pp. 67–68.

repeating the experience of a certain man who went down to Jericho. To create a social civilization requires sober heads, and in this carousal of economic romanticism sober heads were few — the good Samaritan was busy elsewhere.

The doctrine of preëmption and exploitation was reaping its harvest. The frontier spirit was having its splurge, and progress was already turning its face in another direction. Within the next half-century this picturesque America with its heritage of crude energy — greedy, lawless, capable — was to be transformed into a vast uniform middle-class land, dedicated to capitalism and creating the greatest machine-order known to history. A scattered agricultural people, steeped in particularistic jealousies and suspicious of centralization, was to be transformed into an urbanized factory people, rootless, migratory, drawn to the job as by a magnet. It was to come about the more easily because the American farmer had never been a land-loving peasant, rooted to the soil and thriving only in daily contact with familiar acres. He had long been half middle-class, accounting unearned increment the most profitable crop, and buying and selling land as if it were calico. And in consequence the vigorous individualism that had sprung from frontier conditions decayed with the passing of the frontier, and those who had lost in the gamble of preëmption and exploitation were added to the growing multitude of the proletariat. It was from such materials, supplemented by a vast influx of immigrants, that was fashioned the America we know today with its standardized life, its machine culture, its mass psychology — an America to which Jefferson and Jackson and Lincoln would be strangers.

Vernon L. Parrington:

THE AFTERGLOW OF THE
ENLIGHTENMENT—WALT WHITMAN

IF the philosophy of the Enlightenment was fast disintegrating in the America of 1870, it still numbered its picturesque followers who sought to leaven the age with the social spirit of an earlier generation. It was a noble bequest — this gift of the French thinkers — with its passion for liberty, its faith in man, its democratic program. From that great reservoir had come pretty much all that was generously idealistic and humanitarian in the life of the two preceding generations. Its persuasive idealism had woven itself so closely into the fabric of national thought that our fathers had come to believe that America was dedicated in a very special sense to the principles of a free society. The democratic movement returned to it constantly to refresh its strength and take new bearings. At every great crisis the familiar pronouncement of the Declaration of Independence had been confidently appealed to in furtherance of social justice. And now in the days of an acquisitive individualism, when idealism was begging alms in the marketplace, it still threw flashes of romantic splendor on the crude American scene. Old Peter Cooper still dreamed his dreams of social justice after eighty years had passed over his head; and Thaddeus Stevens, grown crabbed and surly from bitter struggles, mutely testified to his passionate equalitarianism on the day of his burial. But it was Walt Whitman in his den at Camden — culturally and in the things of the spirit countless leagues removed from Boston — who was the completest embodiment of the Enlightenment — the poet and prophet of a democracy that the America of the Gilded Age was daily betraying.

In his somewhat truculent pose of democratic undress Whitman was a singular figure for a poet, and especially an American poet. The amplitude and frankness and sincerity of his rich nature were an affront to every polite convention of the day. Endowed with abundant sensuousness and catholic sympathies, he took impressions as sharply as wax from the etcher's hand; and those impressions he transcribed with the careful impartiality of the modern expressionist. His sensitive reactions to experience were emotional rather than intellectual. A pagan, a romantic, a transcendentalist, a mystic — a child of the Enlightenment yet heeding the lessons of science and regarding himself as a realist who honored the physical as the repository of the spiritual — to an amazing degree he was an unconscious embodiment of American aspiration in the days when the romantic revolution was at flood tide. His buoyant nature floated easily on the turbulent stream of national being, and his songs were defiant chants in praise of life — strong, abundant, procreative — flowing through the veins of America.

Oracular and discursive, Whitman lived and moved in a world of sensuous imagery. His imagination was Gothic in its vast reaches. Thronging troops of pictures passed before him, vivid, vital, transcripts of reality, the sharp impress of some experience or fleeting observation — his own and no one's else, and therefore authentic. Delighting in the cosmos he saw reflecting its myriad phases in the mirror of his own ego, he sank into experience joyously like a strong swimmer idling in the salt waves. Borne up by the caressing waters, repressing nothing, rejecting nothing, he found life good in all its manifestations. As an Emersonian he was content to receive his sanctions from within, and as he yielded to the stimulus of the environing present his imagination expanded, his spirits rose to earth's jubilee, his speech fell into lyric cadences, and from the exalted abandon of egoistic experience there issued a strong rich note of the universal. His like had not before appeared in our literature for the reason that the childlike pagan had not before appeared. Emerson with his serene intelligence almost disencumbered of the flesh, and Hawthorne with his desiccating skepticisms that left him afraid of sex, were the fruits of a Hebraized culture that Puritan America understood; but Walt Whitman the caresser of life, the lover who found no sweeter fat than stuck to his own bones, was incomprehensible, and not being understood, it was inevitable that he should be inexorably damned. The most deeply religious soul that American literature knows, the friend and lover of all the world, the

poet of the democratic ideal to which, presumably, America was dedicated, Whitman was flung into outer darkness by the moral custodians of an age that knew morality only from the precepts of the fathers.

The early stages of Whitman's intellectual development are obscure, but that in his twenties he caught most of the infections of the times, literary, political, and social, is clear enough. The young printer-editor in frock coat and tall hat, with cane and boutonnière, who often joined the Bohemian society at Pfaff's restaurant, was a callow romantic, practising the conventional literary arts of the time, writing formal verse, spinning romantic tales,[1] and seeking to approve himself a reputable littérateur. But the passion of reform was already stirring within him and a succession of causes — temperance, anti-capital-punishment, abolitionism — recruited his pen. As a child of Manhattan and of the Jacksonian revolution it was inevitable that his first great passion should have been political, and when in the late forties he found a suitable vehicle of expression in the *Brooklyn Eagle*, his native Jeffersonianism took stock of current political programs. His political master was the radical equalitarian William Leggett — whose praises in after life he never stinted — and from Leggett and the *Evening Post*, supplemented by Fanny Wright and Tom Paine and other disreputable influences, he seems to have got the first clear expression of the sweeping democratic postulates on which later he was to erect his philosophy. The times were stirring everywhere with revolution and on Manhattan Island Locofocoism, with the newfangled matches, ten years before had started its little

[1] See Mabbott, *Short Stories by Walt Whitman*, Columbia University Press, 1927.

local bonfire by way of preparation for a general conflagration that should consume the accumulated mass of wrong and injustice. The ardent young Whitman was deeply infected with Locofoco enthusiasm and his editorials for the *Eagle* were the pronouncements of an extreme left-wing Democrat, as became a disciple of Leggett.

In this early phase of his democracy he fixed his hopes on the great West where, he believed, a freer and more democratic America was taking shape. He was an expansionist, full of ardent hopes, an apostle of "manifest destiny." In such lesser matters as finance and governmental subsidies he was a good Jacksonian, following Old Bullion Benton in his preference for hard money and dislike of shin-plasters. He was opposed to the bankers and monopolists. He called himself a "free-trader by instinct," and so late as 1888 he said, "I object to the tariff primarily because it is not humanitarian — because it is a damnable imposition upon the masses."[2] But these lesser things were inconsequential in comparison with the great objective towards which America was moving — the ever-widening freedom of men in society. "There must be," he wrote in those early years, "continual additions to our great experiment of how much liberty society will bear."[3] On that grand theme he was never tired of speaking. With Tom Paine he believed that just government was a simple thing, fitted to the capacity of many heads; it is made complex to hide its dishonesty. After commenting on the "once derided, but now widely worshipped doctrines which Jefferson and

the glorious Leggett promulgated," he went on:

... this one single rule, rationally construed and applied, is enough to form the starting point of all that is necessary in government: *to make no more laws than those useful for preventing a man or body of men from infringing on the rights of other men.*

And again:

There is not a greater fallacy on earth than the doctrine of *force,* as applied in government. ... Sensible men have long seen that the best government is that which governs least.[4]

Such comments, of course, are only familiar echoes of the Enlightenment — echoes that run through all the thinking of the naturistic school, from Godwin and Paine to Channing and Emerson and Thoreau. In the minds of the children of the Enlightenment the creative ideal of individualism was always pointing toward the ultimate end of philosophic anarchism, and Whitman with his assured faith in the average man accepted the Godwinian political theory as naturally as did Thoreau. What other politics, indeed, was possible for those who built upon the postulates of the innate excellence of human nature and the measureless potentialities of men when vicious social codes have been swept away and the plastic clay is molded by a kindly environment? The perfectibility of man was no romantic dream to the disciples of the French school, but a sober statement of sociological fact, based on a rationalistic psychology; and Whitman was convinced that he was a competent realist in thus envisaging the social problem. If man's instincts are trustworthy, what justification is there for narrow re-

[2] For his late views see Horace Traubel, *With Walt Whitman in Camden,* Vol. 1, p. 99, and elsewhere.

[3] Cleveland Rogers and John Black, *The Gathering of the Forces,* Vol. I, p. 12.

[4] *Ibid.,* Vol. I, pp. 53, 54, 57.

pressions laid on his freedom? Hitherto those repressions have only maimed and distorted him, encouraging his baser rather than his better impulses; and before he can realize his potentialities he must put away all external compulsions and learn to rely solely upon himself. Hence the immediate objective of the democratic revolution was individual freedom, the breaking of all chains, to the end that free men may create a society worthy of them.

So it was as a revolutionary that Whitman began his work; and a revolutionary he remained to the end, although in his last years he chose to call himself an evolutionist. A born rebel, he was always preaching the gospel of rebellion. "I am a radical of radicals," he said late in life, "but I don't belong to any school."[5] It was this revolutionary spirit that made him the friend of all rebellious souls past and present. "My heart is with all you rebels — all of you, today, always, wherever: your flag is my flag,"[6] he said to a Russian anarchist; and it was this sympathy that enabled him to understand Fanny Wright and Tom Paine and Priestley, who "have never had justice done them."[7] "The future belongs to the radical," and so Leaves of Grass — he says in "Starting from Paumanok" — "beat the gong of revolt." Conventional law and order he frankly despised and those individuals who sought their own law and followed it awoke his admiration. Thoreau's "lawlessness" delighted him — "his going his own absolute road let hell blaze all it chooses." It is a coward and a poltroon who accepts his law from others — as true of communities as it is true of individuals. He was a good Jeffer-

sonian in his fear of Federalistic consolidation that must put an end to local rights and freedoms.

> To the States or any one of them, or any city
>   of the States,
>   *Resist much, obey little,*
> Once unquestioning obedience, once fully
>   enslaved,
> . . . no nation, state, city of this earth, ever
>   afterward resumes its liberty.[8]

> I am for those that have never been master'd,
> For men and women whose tempers have
>   never been master'd,
> For those whom laws, theories, conventions
>   can never master.[9]

This is the spirit of the radical forties when men were prone to repudiate their allegiance to the political state; when left-wing Abolitionists were dissolving the Union by resolutions; and transcendentalists were proclaiming the doctrine of nullification of unrighteous law. It had come out of the Jacksonian upheaval, but it was daily discovering fresh sanctions as the anarchistic premises of the Enlightenment were more adequately explored and the revolutionary spirit of Europe broke in upon America. During these turbulent years Whitman's great plan was in gestation, but before *Leaves of Grass* came to print in the first slender edition of 1855 other influences had been at work, confirming his earlier views, endowing them with lyric passion and expanding them into a grandiose whole. Those influences would seem to have been the fervid emotionalism of the fifties, the monistic idealism of the transcendental school, and the emerging

---

5 Traubel, *op. cit.*, Vol. I, p. 215.

6 *Ibid.*, Vol. I, p. 65.

7 *Ibid.*, Vol. I, pp. 79–80.

8 *Leaves of Grass*, inclusive edition ed. by Emory Halloway, Garden City, N. Y., 1927. Hereafter called *Leaves*. "To the States," p. 8.

9 *Ibid.*, "By Blue Ontario's Shore," p. 297, ll. 21–23.

scientific movement. On the whole perhaps it was the first, with its vague and expansive Utopianism, that bit most deeply, stimulating his rich pagan nature to unconventional frankness and encouraging him to throw off the inhibitions of a Puritan ethicism that held American thought in narrow bondage. The rude and ample liberalisms that so shocked his early readers were in no sense peculiar to Whitman, despite common opinion, but the expression of the surging emotionalism of the times, and *Leaves of Grass,* can best be understood by setting its frank paganism against the background of the lush fifties.

With its Calvinistic antecedents — Scotch-Irish and Huguenot as well as New England Puritan — America had always been unfriendly to a pagan evaluation of man's duties and destiny, and the revolutionary movement of the forties had been kept within sober ethical bounds. John Humphrey Noyes was probably the most radical American of the times, yet the Perfectionism of his earlier years, with its ascetic religiosity, bore little resemblance to the later communism of the Oneida Community. But the liberalism of the fifties was casting off all Hebraic restraints and running wild, proclaiming a new heaven about to appear on the free continent of America, and bidding the youth of the land live joyously as children of the earth. Paganism for the first time lifted up its head and surveyed the American scene — a youthful paganism, lusty and vigorous, that suggested amazing applications of the respectable doctrines of freedom and individuality, to the scandal of older-fashioned folk. From the free spaces of the West, carried on the tide of the Gold Rush, had come a spontaneous reaction from the earlier repressions. Liberalism

was passing from the political to the social — a free welling-up of repressed desires, a vast expansiveness. Too long had the natural human emotions been under the ban of asceticism; too long had a God of wrath dispossessed a God of love. Life is good in the measure that it is lived fully, and to live fully is to live in the flesh as well as the spirit. Emerson the prophet of the earlier decade had suffered from an extreme unfleshliness; Whitman the prophet of the fifties would recover the balance. As the current of emotionalism gathered force a frank *joie de vivre* submerged the old reticences; candor, frankness, a very lust of self-expression, was the new law for free men and women — a glorification of the physical that put to rout the traditional Hebraisms. A riotous sentimentalism ran about the land until it seemed to timid souls as if liberty were quite running away with decency. Freedom for black slaves was one thing, but freedom for women — the loosening of social convention — suggested terrifying eventualities like free love and the disruption of the family. They would countenance no such immoral freedom and under the leadership of young Anthony Comstock the forces of reticence and respectability made ready to do battle with the new liberalisms.

It was not alone Walt Whitman who threw down the gage to the Comstockian watchmen in the gates. The apostle of the new freedom, the high priest of emotional liberalism, was Henry Ward Beecher, lately come out of the West, who from the pulpit of Plymouth Church swept his thousands of idolizing followers along the path of Utopian emotionalism. With a rich amplitude and golden vagueness of metaphor he preached the new gospel. From his lips flowed a lyric chant, a vast paean, a very shout in

praise of liberty and love, of godlike
man and a manlike God. "Life — affirma-
tive, immediate, in a highly ornamented
Mayday world — he acknowledged and
commemorated life!"[10] He bathed in a
"perpetual tropical luxuriance of blessed
love." "I never knew how to worship
until I knew how to love," he cried; "and
to love I must have something . . . that
touching my heart, shall not leave the
chill of ice but the warmth of summer."
Like a good Emersonian he discarded
reason — the discipline of the ancestral
Calvinism — to follow the "secret chords
of feeling," the "heart's instincts, whose
channels you may appoint but whose
flowing is beyond control." A "magnificent pagan" — so Thoreau called him —
he reveled in sensuous beauty. His emotions mounted as he contemplated this
new land, this new people, the golden
future that beckoned — with all shackles
broken, dedicated to freedom, warm and
palpitating from abundant life — a radiant world of lovely women and manly
men. He dwelt on Pisgah and from the
heights looked out on a divine democracy. "The life of the common people is
the best part of the world's life," he ex-
claimed; "the life of the common people
is the life of God." And to his congrega-
tion intoxicated with his rhetoric he
shouted, "Ye are gods! You are crystal-
line, your faces are radiant!"[11] And the
end and outcome envisaged by this
prophet of the American Idea was a
vaguely grandiose fellowship, not of the
Saints alone, but of all the thronging
children of men, for of such is God's
kingdom of this world.

As such lyric chants fell on Whitman's
ears, they must have quickened the fer-
ment of thought that was eventually to

clarify for him the ideal of democracy,
exalting it by making it warm and human
and social. The old Jacksonian leveling
had been negative; its freedoms had been
individual; its anarchism selfish and un-
social. The great ideal of the fellowship
had been lost in the scramble for rights.
Even transcendental democracy had narrowed its contacts. The hermit Thoreau
in his cabin at Walden Pond was no
symbol of a generous democratic future.
In the struggle for liberty and equality
the conception of fraternity had been
denied and the golden trinity of the
Enlightenment dismembered. It was this
idea of fraternity, made human and
hearty by his warm love of men and
women, that Whitman got from the expansive fifties and built into his thinking.
The conception of solidarity, then entering the realm of proletarian thought
through the labors of Friedrich Engels
and Karl Marx, was his response to the
new times — a response that infused his
democratic faith with a glowing human-
ism. Democracy spiritualized by Channing and Emerson and Parker had
suffered limitations from their lingering
Hebraisms — the Puritan passion for
righteousness had imposed strict ethical
bounds on the democratic will. In
Thoreau it had been subjected to caustic
skepticisms — the transcendental individ-
ualist quizzically asked, "What *is* your
people?" and refused to subject himself
to the mass. But in Whitman all limitations and skepticisms were swept away
by the feeling of comradeship. Flesh is
kin to flesh, and out of the great reserves
of life is born the average man "with his
excellent good manliness." Not in distinction but in oneness with the whole
is found the good life, for in fellowship
is love and in the whole is freedom; and
love and freedom are the law and the
prophets. The disintegrations of the
earlier individualism must be succeeded

---

[10] Constance Mayfield Rourke, *Trumpets of Jubilee*, p. 171.

[11] *Ibid.*, p. 172.

by a new integration; fear and hate and jealousy and pride have held men apart hitherto, but love will draw them together. After all solidarity — the children of America merging in the fellowship, sympathetic, responsive, manlike yet divine, of which the poet should be the prophet and literature provide the sermons.

It was a noble conception — washing away all the meanness that befouled Jacksonian individualism — and it somewhat slowly found its way to parity with his first master conception, the universal ego, and settled into place in those later opening lines of *Leaves of Grass:*

One's-self I sing, a simple separate person,
Yet utter the word Democratic, the word
  En-Masse.[12]

Then came the war to strengthen his faith in the common man. As he watched the soldiers marching, fighting, suffering, he was deeply impressed with their courage, patience, kindness, manliness, and came to reverence the deep wellspring of national being from which issued such inexhaustible waters. It was not the few but the many that gave him hope. "I never before so realized the majesty and reality of the American people *en masse*," he wrote of some regiments returning from the front. "It fell upon me like a great awe."[13] And as he contemplated this fecund people, with its sons and daughters issuing strong and wholesome from every part of the land, there came to him a new conception of unity — the Union that Lincoln loved — the drawing together into an indissoluble whole of the far-flung commonwealths — a realization of the perfect State where reign liberty, equality, fraternity. Solidarity

had taken on a political complexion but its life-blood was in the veins of a free people.

But pagan though he was in his deeper nature, a child of the emotional fifties, he was a transcendentalist also and his democratic philosophy, as it took shape, bears unmistakable marks of the New England school, supplemented perhaps by Quakerism. His well-known comment, "I was simmering and simmering; it was Emerson brought me to boil," suggests much, and in particular that the Enlightenment as it had come to him through the Jeffersonian heritage was supplemented and spiritualized by the Enlightenment as it had taken special form in passing through the transcendental mind. To this latter source must be traced the philosophic monism that served to draw his speculations together — a mystic sense of the divine oneness of life that took his major postulates in golden hands and fused them into a single spiritual whole. Thus instructed the "great Idea, the idea of perfect and free individuals," became curiously Emersonian in all its amplifications. There is the same glorification of consciousness and will, the same exaltation of the soul, the same trust in the buried life that men call instinct, the same imperious call to heed the voice of innate Godhood; and round and about this "perfect and free individual" is a mystical egocentric universe wherein the children of men may luxuriate in their divinity. The body is excellent as the soul is excellent; away, therefore, with all shamefacedness — the mean secretiveness, the putting of fingers to the lips in presence of the naked, the lies in presence of open palpable fact! For if this be indeed God's universe, and He is in and through it all, the children of Adam may stand in His presence unafraid — nay, rather with pride in their own excellence. "I exist as I am, that is enough," for "Divine

12 *Leaves*, "One's-Self I Sing," p. 1, ll. 1–2.

13 *Autobiographia*, p. 73. See also *Democratic Vistas*, p. 74.

am I inside and out, and I make holy whatever I touch or am touch'd from."

Whitman not only accepted Emerson with ungrudging loyalty but he dwelt much with Hegel and the German idealists, and with their help he penetrated curiously to the core of things, discovering there an inner spiritual reality that is the abiding substance behind the external manifestation. He had come upon food to sustain his faith in presence of the mean and base that compassed him about, and the puzzling contradictions of life no longer troubled him. If man be perfectible, if he be indeed a child of God though still in his infancy, how glorious must be the future toward which he is pressing! The evil will pass and the good remain.

Roaming in thought over the Universe, I saw
    the little that is Good steadily hastening
    towards immortality,
And the vast all that is call'd Evil I saw
    hastening to merge itself and become
    lost and dead.[14]

When he turned from the oracular utterance of *Leaves of Grass* to sober exposition, he phrased it thus:

There is, apart from mere intellect . . . a wondrous something that realises without argument . . . an intuition of the absolute balance, in time and space, of the whole of this multifarious, mad chaos of fraud, frivolity, hoggishness — this revel of fools, and incredible make-believe and general unsettledness, we call the *world;* a soul-sight of that divine clue and unseen thread which holds the whole congeries of things, all history and time, and all events however trivial, however momentous, like a leash'd dog in the hands of the hunter.[15]

To discover this divine clue and be drawn by the unseen thread into the orbit of things, to suffer the Me — the "human identity of understanding, emotions, spirit" — to fuse with the Not Me — "the whole of the material, objective universe and laws, with what is behind them in time and space" — became therefore for Whitman the grand objective of man's life and effort. This for him was the sum and substance of religion, which was no other than the binding of the individual back upon the whole. "A vast similitude interlocks all." And so from his conception of social solidarity he went forward to the conception of spiritual solidarity, and discovered religion to be the crown and glory of the "American Idea." Walt Whitman and America were to be the prophets of religion. "Easily at home in a natural world of prodigious brightness and scale, he . . . saw 'the most splendid race the sun ever shone upon,' and was urging the life of instinct and impulse. Love was the key — taking form and in 'Starting from Paumanok' he asserted his Love, Democracy, Religion — a new religion."[16] His message was purpose.

The soul,
Forever and forever — longer than soil is
    brown and solid — longer than water
    ebbs and flows.

I will make the poems of materials, for I
    think they are to be the most spiritual
    poems,
And I will make the poems of my body and
    of mortality,
For I think I shall then supply myself with
    the poems of my soul and of immortality.

I will make a song for these States that no
    one State may under any circumstances
    be subjected to another State,
    · · · · · · ·
I will sing the song of companionship,
    · · · · · · ·

14 *Leaves,* "Roaming in Thought," p. 233.
15 "Carlyle from the American Point of View," in *Specimen Days, Prose Works,* pp. 174–175.
16 Rourke, *op. cit.,* p. 173.

I will write the evangel-poem of comrades
    and of love,

. . . .

I am the credulous man of qualities, ages,
    races,
I advance from the people in their own spirit,

. . . .

I, too, following many and follow'd by many,
    inaugurate a religion, . . .

. . . .

Each is not for its own sake,
I say the whole earth and all the stars in the
    sky are for religion's sake.

I say no man has ever yet been half devout
    enough,
None has ever yet adored or worship'd half
    enough,
None has begun to think how divine he him-
    self is, and how certain the future is.

I say that the real and permanent grandeur
    of these States must be their religion,
Otherwise there is no real and permanent
    grandeur;

. . . .

My comrade!
For you to share with me two greatnesses,
    and a third one rising inclusive and
    more resplendent,
The greatness of Love and Democracy, and
    the greatness of Religion.[17]

But this new religion of the mystical
Whitman, in harmony with post-tran-
scendental thought, was deeply impreg-
nated with the spirit of science. He was
in the very fullness of his powers when
the conception of evolution came to him
and he greeted it gladly, weaving it into
all his thinking and discovering in it a
confirmation of his idealistic philosophy.
It was the evolution of Herbert Spencer,
it must be remembered, that Whitman
accepted — teleological, buoyantly optimistic, dominated by the conception of

progress, shot through with the spirit of
the Enlightenment; and such an evolution was a confirmation and not a denial
of his transcendental premises. It supplemented rather than contradicted the
tenets of his faith. Like Emerson as he
saw the bounds of the material universe
slowly pushed back by science he discovered amidst the constant change
the presence of growth, development, the
natural passage from the simple to the
complex; and like Theodore Parker he
felt that this slow unfolding was no other
than the unfolding of God, making Himself evident and unmistakable to man.
Evolution was God's great plan. "The law
over all, the law of laws, is the law of
successions," he was persuaded; "for
what is the present after all but a growth
out of the past?" But noble as is the
evidence of God's work discoverable by
science, the soul is not content to rest
with such evidence; it must seek out the
reality behind the manifestation; and for
this work the poet alone is fitted. The
poet must complete the work of the
scientist. The noble "Passage to India" is
a lovely chant of human progress, the
adventurous soul conquering the earth;
but it must not pause there; it must seek
God through the universe until it finds
Him, and "Nature and Man shall be dis-
join'd and diffused no more," and "All
these hearts as of fretted children shall
be sooth'd."

Bathe me O God in thee, mounting to thee,
I and my soul to range in range of thee.[18]

It was in this profoundly religious
spirit that Whitman accepted science,
built it into his poetry, rested confidently
upon it; and it is this spirit that explains
his formal statement in the "Song of
Myself."

[17] *Leaves,* "Starting from Paumanok," p. 14,
ll. 22–26; p. 15, ll. 1, 13, 19, 22–23; p. 16, ll. 2,
5–11; p. 17, ll. 7–10.

[18] *Leaves,* p. 349, ll. 18–19.

I accept Reality and dare not question it,
Materialism first and last imbuing.

Hurrah for positive science! long live exact
    demonstration!
Fetch stonecrop mixt with cedar and
    branches of lilac,
This is the lexicographer, this the chemist,
    this made a grammar of the old
    cartouches,
These mariners put the ship through danger-
    ous unknown seas,
This the geologist, this works with the
    scalpel, and this is the mathematician.

Gentlemen, to you the first honors always!
Your facts are useful, and yet they are not
    my dwelling,
I but enter by them to an area of my
    dwelling.[19]

Equipped with such a philosophy and
supported by such a faith Whitman accepted the twin duties laid upon him:
to make clear to America her present
failure in the great adventure — how far
she had fallen short hitherto of any adequate democratic reality; and to mark
out afresh the path to the Canaan of
democratic hopes — reviving the early
hopes of the Enlightenment and drawing
in lovelier colors the democratic Utopia
dreamed of for a hundred years. To be
both critic and prophet — that he conceived to be his mission, a mission that
he was faithful to for upwards of forty
years. For the first duty he was admirably equipped. No other knew this America so intimately or so broadly — had
penetrated so lovingly to the common
heart and read so clearly its secret hopes
and fears. That America was not yet a
democracy — was very far indeed from
a democracy — that it was a somewhat
shoddy *bourgeois* capitalistic society shot
through with cant and hypocrisy and

every meanness, he saw with calm,
searching eyes. No contemporary critic,
not Godkin, not Emerson, saw more
clearly the unlovely reality or dealt with
it more scathingly, not only in *Leaves of
Grass* but especially in his prose writings
and in casual talk. . . .[20]

As a realist Whitman granted the worst
charges of the critics of democracy, but
he probed deeper and brought other
facts to light that modified the equation.
It was the difficult question the old Fed-
eralists had posed and that Carlyle had
lately revived — the question, is not this
meanness inseparable from democracy?
is not your people in fact a great beast,
requiring the lash and the curb? It was
the crux of the long debate over democracy and to it Whitman gave anxious and
frequent consideration. In fighting the
battle of 1790 over again, like Jefferson
he rested his case on the native integrity
and measureless potentiality of the "bulk-
people" — they are the deep soil from
which spring the abundant fruits and
flowers of civilization. Gentle-nurtured
folk do not understand this — they do not
like the rank qualities of vital being.
Matthew Arnold "always gives you the
notion that he hates to touch the dirt —
the dirt is so dirty! But everything comes
out of the dirt — everything: everything
comes out of the people . . . not university people, not F.F.V. people: people,
people, just people!" In the rude, vital,
natural man is the inexhaustible wellspring of good and evil; "He's got it all
. . . not only the cruel, beastly, hoggish,
cheating, bedbug qualities, but also the
spiritual — the noble — the high-born";[21]
in "some ways" he is a "devil of a fellow,"
but he is not "all devil or even chiefly

---

[19] *Leaves*, p. 43, ll. 9–17.

[20] [Here is omitted an illustrative passage from
Democratic Vistas. — Ed.]

[21] Traubel, *op. cit.*, Vol. I, p. 174.

devil."[22] And because he is not chiefly devil such love and beauty and justice and comradeship as there is in the world, such progress in civilization as has been made hitherto, have been possible — how otherwise? If he has journeyed thus far out of the primeval slime, what bounds shall be set to his eventual journeyings? Why put out one's eyes with a mere handful of years?

So Whitman projected his democratic commonwealth far into the future; he would not have us believe that it had been realized here in America. Political democracy, the struggle for political rights that had engaged America hitherto, was only negative, a necessary preliminary to the ultimate reality. "I submit," he said, "that the fruition of democracy, on aught like a grand scale, resides altogether in the future," and its realization depends upon the use to which the people put their freedom. If from it emerges a proud and self-conscious individualism — "the quality of Being, in the object's self, according to its own central idea and purpose, and of growing therefrom and thereto — not criticism by other standards, and adjustments thereto" — then democracy on a grand scale will be possible and the self-reliant citizen will take his place in a free creative society. The ideal of the growing man, and the ideal of the perfect State — broadly social rather than narrowly political — these were his twin ideals; and the tie that is to bind men together in spontaneous solidarity is love. How characteristic is his sketch of the perfect city, and how deeply saturated with the Enlightenment! There is wanting only a physiocratic economics to make it perfect.

A great city is that which has the greatest men and women,

. . . .

Where the city stands with the brawniest breed of orators and bards,
Where the city stands that is belov'd by these, and loves them in return and understands them,
Where no monuments exist to heroes but in the common words and deeds,
Where thrift is in its place, and prudence is in its place,
Where the men and women think lightly of the laws,
Where the slave ceases and the master of slaves ceases,
Where the populace rise at once against the never-ending audacity of elected persons,

. . . .

Where outside authority enters always after the precedence of inside authority,
Where the citizen is always the head and ideal, and President, Mayor, Governor and what not, are agents for pay,
Where children are taught to be laws to themselves, and to depend on themselves,
Where equanimity is illustrated in affairs,

. . . .

Where the city of faithfulest friends stands,
Where the city of the cleanliness of the sexes stands,

. . . .

There the great city stands.[23]

Individualism, solidarity — on such strong bases he erected his ideal democracy, and the heaven-reaching temple will be overlaid with the rich arts and graces of a civilization worthy at last of the name. Such was the Enlightenment as it came to flower in the passionate idealism of Walt Whitman — a dream that was mocked and flouted and nullified by the Drews and Fisks and Goulds — the "hoggish, cheating, bedbug qualities" of a generation that scorned him for a beast. Even his stout faith was shaken at times by the infidelities of the Gilded

---

[22] *Ibid.*, Vol. I, p. 285.

[23] *Leaves*, "Song of the Broad Axe," p. 160, ll. 7, 14–20, 21–22; p. 161, ll. 1–2, 6–7, 10.

Age. He was troubled by the gap that opened between the free individual and the perfect State. "I seem to be reaching for a new politics — for a new economy," he confessed in 1888; "I don't quite know what, but for something."[24] Although he protested, "The older I grow . . . the more I am confirmed in my optimism, my democracy," he projected his hopes farther into the future. He sympathized with the socialists but he was not one of them. His revolutionary ardor abated and he preferred in later years to call himself an evolutionist.[25] "Be radical — be radical," he said to Traubel, "be not too damned radical."[26] With his catholic sympathies that refused all bitterness he could not be a partisan — "after the best the partisan will say something better will be said by the man."[27]

So in the twilight of the romantic revolution Whitman quietly slipped away. The great hopes on which he fed have been belied by after events — so his critics say;[28] as the great hopes of the Enlightenment have been belied. Certainly in this welter of today, with science become the drab and slut of war and industrialism, with sterile money-slaves instead of men, Whitman's expansive hopes seem grotesque enough. Democracy may indeed be only a euphemism for the rulership of fools. Yet in a time of huge infidelities, in the dun breakdown and disintegration of all faiths, it is not wholly useless to recall the large proportions of Walt Whitman, his tenderness, his heartiness, his faith, his hope. There was in him no weak

evasion, no sniveling over the shards of the goodly vessel broken at the well, but even when "old, alone, sick, weak-down, melted-worn with sweat," a free and joyous acceptance of life.

Thanks in old age — thanks ere I go,.
For health, the midday sun, the impalpable air — for life, mere life,
    . . . . . .
For all my days — not those of peace alone — the days of war the same,
For gentle words, caresses, gifts from foreign lands,
For shelter, wine and meat — for sweet appreciation,
    . . . . . .
For beings, groups, love, deeds, words, books — for colors, forms,
For all the brave strong men — devoted, hardy, men — who've forward sprung in freedom's help, all years, all lands,
For braver, stronger, more devoted men — (a special laurel ere I go, to life's war's chosen ones,
The cannoneers of song and thought — the great artillerists — the foremost leaders, captains of the soul:)
As soldier from an ended war return'd — As traveler out of myriads, to the long procession retrospective,
Thanks — joyful thanks! — a soldier's, traveler's thanks.[29]

A great figure, the greatest assuredly in our literature — yet perhaps only a great child — summing up and transmitting into poetry all the passionate aspiration of an America that had passed through the romantic revolution, the poet of selfhood and the prophet of brotherhood, the virile man and the catholic lover — how shall Walt Whitman become dumb or cease to speak to men unless the children of those who are now half-devil and half-God shall prove to be wholly devil — or wholly moron?

24 Traubel, *op. cit.*, Vol. I, p. 101.

25 *Ibid.*, Vol. I, pp. 193, 215.

26 *Ibid.*, Vol. I, p. 223.

27 *Ibid.*, Vol. I, p. 363.

28 See Norman Foerster, *American Criticism*, pp. 211–222; Lucy Lockwood Hazard, *The Frontier in American Literature*, pp. 170–177.

29 *Leaves*, "Thanks in Old Age," p. 435.

Ralph Henry Gabriel:

THE GOSPEL OF WEALTH
OF THE GILDED AGE

WHEN his war-time ambassadorship in England came to an end, Charles Francis Adams returned to a new and strange America. He was astonished at some of the changes. "Most noticeable of these," he remarked in 1871, "is perhaps to be found in a greatly enlarged grasp of enterprise and increased facility of combination. The great operations of war, the handling of large masses of men, the influence of discipline, the lavish expenditure of unprecedented sums of money, the immense financial operations, the possibilities of effective co-operation were lessons not likely to be lost on men quick to receive and to apply all new ideas."[1] Adams recognized, however, that it was not the war alone that had brought in the new day.

A concatenation of events in the 1850's and 1860's initiated an industrial revolution in the United States. Previous to the fall of Sumter, states in the northeast quarter of the nation had been exploring their natural resources with scientific aid; during the same period the federal government had occasionally sent expeditions into wilderness areas to map the boundaries of mineral beds. The successors of Father Hennepin and Sieur La Salle had determined the extent and quality of the copper fields of Michigan; they had studied the more important eastern bituminous coal fields; and had brought to light the astounding wealth of iron ore which nature had thoughtfully placed so near the surface of the ground beside the shores of Lake Superior. Coal and iron are twin foundations of an industrial civilization. By the end of the Civil War, Americans recognized that the nation possessed both minerals in almost unlimited amounts. It was possible for the ambitious entrepreneur of the mid-nineteenth century to visualize the manner in which coal and iron could be brought together. Since the beginning of their national history, Americans had been a people scattered over a vast area. By constructing turnpikes, steamboats for lakes and rivers, and canals, they had partly solved their peculiar problems of great distances. But the railroad was the first development in transportation which offered the possibility of breaking down the semi-isolation of the sections and of transforming the nation into a single economic unit. Sufficient technical advance in railway construction had been made before Lincoln's inauguration to make possible the conquest of the Appalachians and the linking of the Upper

[1] *North American Review*, April, 1871, CXII, 243.

Mississippi Valley to the Atlantic sea-board. The perfection of the air brake in 1868 marked the beginning of the modern railroad. Both railways and industry needed cheap steel and, in the 1850's, Bessemer in England and Kelly in America devised methods for making it. With the consolidation of Bessemer and Kelly interests in the United States in 1866, the age of steel and of the steam engine began. Almost at once bituminous coal surpassed water as the principal source of power for American factories. The preservation of the Union by war made possible the exploitation of the resources of America without the hampering conditions which would have attended the establishment of new international boundaries. The surrender of Lee meant that Americans could build their industrial civilization on a vaster scale than was possible in the nineteenth century for any other nation.

Before Grant's artillery had been hauled for the last time off Virginia battlefields, a number of American entrepreneurs had begun to demonstrate what free men could accomplish in such a country as the United States. The five years which succeeded the war, continued Adams bitterly, "have witnessed some of the most remarkable examples of organized lawlessness, under the forms of law, which mankind has yet had an opportunity to study. If individuals have, as a rule, quietly pursued their peaceful vocations, the same cannot be said of certain single men at the head of vast combinations of private wealth. This has been particularly the case as regards those controlling the rapidly developed railroad interests. These modern potentates have declared war, negotiated peace, reduced courts, legislatures, and sovereign States to an unqualified obedience to their will, disturbed trade, agitated the currency, imposed taxes, and, boldly setting both law and public opinion at defiance, have freely exercised many other attributes of sovereignty. . . . Single men have controlled hundreds of miles of railway, thousands of men, tens of millions of revenue, and hundreds of millions of capital. The strength implied in all this they wielded in practical independence of the control both of governments and of individuals; much as petty German despots might have governed their little principalities a century or two ago."[2]

Adams recorded only the beginning of the story; by the end of the century the machine age for America had come into being. Primitive technology had become developed technology. Small business had become big business. The old-time individual entrepreneur, who worked shoulder to shoulder with his help, had been replaced by the large corporation as the significant factor in industrial and commercial advance. And competition had been modified by the development of monopolistic tendencies. Americans, once divided on sectional lines, became increasingly conscious of a new grouping and tended to think of themselves as farmers, wage earners, or industrialists and business men. The immigrant stream across the north Atlantic swelled to the largest folk movement in modern history. Great urban centers appeared and sprawled without plan each year farther from their original centers. The frontier passed. The Old World suddenly became conscious that an industrial giant had appeared in North America and was squinting eastward and westward across the oceans to see what profits could be made abroad.

The preachers of the romantic democratic faith of pre-Sumter days were fond

[2] *Ibid.*, April, 1871, CXII, 244.

of pointing out that Providence had reserved America for the growth of civil liberty, and that, without the hampering restrictions of ecclesiastical or political autocracy or of a feudal aristocratic system, democracy had been able to raise its beacon in the New World. They might have added that Providence appeared to have scattered prodigious natural wealth throughout the area of the United States and dug on either side a moat of ocean width in order that the institution of industrial capitalism might have an opportunity to demonstrate the gifts it could bring to men. Never since it originated in the ancient world had that institution developed in so rich an environment with so few legal or political restrictions. In June, 1889, Andrew Carnegie, who had risen from the post of bobbin boy to become one of the greatest of the new luminaries in the American industrial sky, contributed to the *North American Review* what its editor declared to be "the finest article I have ever published in the *Review*."[3] The title of the piece was "Wealth."

The Carnegie essay was a formulation of a philosophy for the new era, a "Gospel of Wealth." It was not, however, the only philosophy of the period. Jay Gould, Jim Fisk, and Daniel Drew were among the prophets of the gospel of grab and hold. They represented what Thorstein Veblen later called the hawk influence of pecuniary competition. But all industrial capitalism was affected by this influence. Competition implied conflict, and conflict expressed itself in such stratagems as flank marches, surprise attacks, and even frontal assaults. The war of the market place was costly, with the result that the tendency toward the development of local peace areas, called "trusts," became almost irresistible. A later generation has called the decades which immediately followed Appomattox the age of the "robber barons." They were a primitive company of chieftains recruited for the most part from the ranks of the humble people. Some of them accumulated such power as no American had hitherto known. Their number included men who dreamed of building empires and who came near to transforming their visions into realities.

These new industrial Brobdingnags, who brought together capital, labor, and machines, were governed, particularly in the early phases of their activities, by what was expedient — for them. By 1900 most of these leaders had become convinced that what was expedient for them was best for the country. They had, moreover, no choice but to follow an ethics of expediency, if they would survive as individuals. The mores of a simpler agricultural and commercial era did not fit the conditions of an age characterized by the swift accumulation of industrial power. The new chieftains created not only new techniques of exploitation, of promotion, and of management, but also new customs and a new mental outlook.

Out of this turbulent, swiftly moving transition period came what Carnegie called the gospel of wealth. He apparently used the term to distinguish his formula from the discipline of economics which young John Bates Clark had called, a short time before, the science of wealth. But the king of steel had little to do with originating the gospel he preached; he merely formulated a philosophy as universal in the United States as smoke in Pittsburgh.

The congeries of social beliefs which he called the gospel of wealth stemmed primarily from the *laissez-faire* attitude

[3] Quoted in B. J. Hendrick, *The Life of Andrew Carnegie*, 1932, I, 330. Quoted with the permission of Doubleday, Doran & Company.

of the nineteenth century. The mercantilistic assumptions conditioning the thought of the Fathers of the Constitution had been reduced vastly in importance by the time Franklin Pierce came to the White House. There was then no regulation of industry by the nation, save in the uncertain and shifting tariff policy, and almost no interference by the states. In pre-Sumter decades, when the small entrepreneur was the typical American industrialist, *laissez faire* was more a condition than a theory. Its important theoretical formulation did not come until big business had been subjected to assaults by both farmers and wage earners. The date, 1889, of Carnegie's essay is not without significance. It followed the revolt of the Grangers by more than a decade and a half. Twelve years before it appeared had occurred the railway strikes of the frightening summer of 1878. It was written three years after the Haymarket Riot in Chicago, the signal for a nation-wide crusade against anarchism. Its timing suggests that it was an apologia. In spite of the evidence to support this contention, the hypothesis does not seem to fit the facts. Carnegie formulated a folk philosophy which was not only being accepted, but was being acted upon by the farmers who joined the Grange and by the more able and ambitious laboring men who looked forward hopefully to individual advancement to the status of property owners. The steelmaster gave words to an economic philosophy which was dominant in the United States of the Gilded Age. It was an elaboration of the doctrine of the free individual of the American democratic faith and was a result of the discovery that this tenet had important utilities in the new industrial capitalism.

The American gospel of wealth of the Gilded Age was erected upon a theory of property which had its most elaborate development in that Scottish common-sense philosophy dominating the intellectual atmosphere of most American colleges and universities in the decades immediately following Appomattox. This system of thought, in the opinion of its great American leaders, Presidents James McCosh of Princeton and Noah Porter of Yale, made it possible for Christianity to escape the pitfalls hidden within the idealism of Bishop Berkeley, of Immanuel Kant, and of Ralph Waldo Emerson, and to come to grips with a real world of matter and men. The shadow of John Calvin lay across the formulas of common sense. "Each individual man," affirmed Noah Porter in 1884, ". . . has separate wants of body and spirit, to the supply of which he is impelled by original impulses of instinct and rational desire. . . . The supply of many of the wants of men implies the existence of property." Man's Creator, then, has laid upon him a duty to acquire property and to defend it, once it has come into his possession. The right of the individual to his property and the duty of the State to assist him in its defense is clear. Property rights derive from a higher law than that made by men. "Governments exist very largely — in the view of many, they exist solely — for the purpose of rendering this service [of defending rights in property]."[4] Porter would put the sanction of religion behind property rights. "God has bestowed upon us certain powers and gifts which no one is at liberty to take from us or to interfere with," affirmed James McCosh in 1892. "All attempts to deprive us of them is theft. Under the same head may be placed all purposes to deprive us of the right to earn property or to use it as we see fit."[5]

[4] Noah Porter, *Elements of Moral Science*, 1885, 362, 368.

[5] James McCosh, *Our Moral Nature*, 1892, 40.

The corollary of the divine right of property was the acquisition of wealth by industry and thrift. This latter doctrine was not new. In America it ran back to seventeenth century Puritanism. A godly man, said Cotton Mather, one Sabbath day in the early eighteenth century, must have two callings: his general calling and his personal calling. The first is, of course, "to serve the Lord Jesus Christ"; the second is "a certain *Particular Employment*, by which his Usefulness in his neighborhood is distinguished." "A Christian, at his *Two Callings*," Mather added, "is a man in a Boat, Rowing for Heaven; the House which our Heavenly Father hath intended for us. If he mind but one of his *Callings*, be it which it will, he pulls the *oar*, but on one side of the Boat, and it will make but a poor dispatch to the Shoar of Eternal Blessedness."[6] To be diligent in one's earthly calling was, then, a moral duty, a precept of that fundamental law basic to the theories of Calvinism, and later of the democratic faith. To produce with energy but to consume sparingly and to the glory of God was the seventeenth century Puritan doctrine sanctifying work and thrift. It was preached in the eighteenth century throughout the land by the Deist, Benjamin Franklin, creator of "Poor Richard." It was caught up by Francis Asbury and in the nineteenth century spread by his Methodist circuit riders throughout the continental interior. Its advice to the young man was: work and save, if you would win the game of life and honor the God who made you. "Work for the Night is Coming" became a popular hymn of evangelical Protestantism.

When industrialism began after 1865 the creation of a new world, this Puritan code of worldly asceticism sprang into new importance. It had served well in a day when the wilderness was stubborn and when laborers were few. Then it had been a religious sanction behind inevitable frontier mores. But when Americans began the exploitation of the richest mineral resources of the world, the old doctrine began to have new uses. "By the proper use of wealth," wrote D. S. Gregory, author of a textbook on ethics used during the 1880's in many American colleges, "man may greatly elevate and extend his moral work. It is therefore his duty to seek to secure wealth for this high end, and to make a diligent use of what the Moral Governor may bestow upon him for the same end. . . . The Moral Governor has placed the power of acquisitiveness in man for a good and noble purpose. . . ."[7]

Better even than the formulation of the doctrine of property by the presidents of Princeton and of Yale, or even of Professor Gregory, was that of the head of Williams College. Mark Hopkins, like Emerson, was an old man when Lee surrendered. The great period of the two coincided. Both had last words after Appomattox. Hopkins carried forward into the new era the best tradition of evangelical Protestantism. He published in 1868 a treatise on ethics, entitled significantly, *The Law of Love and Love as Law*. The authentic voice of evangelicalism sounded through the book. Its very title suggests the change brought by romanticism during the Middle Period to American Christianity. The hardness of Calvinism had been softened. The old fear of God had relaxed. Love had been substituted for discipline. Hopkins set his theory of property against the background of a law of love. "The Right to Property," said the aging Hopkins in

[6] Cotton Mather, *Two Brief Discourses, one directing a Christian in his General Calling; another directing him in his Personal Calling,* 1701, 37–38.

[7] Daniel Seely Gregory, *Christian Ethics,* 1875, 224.

1868, "reveals itself through an original desire. The affirmation of it is early and universally made, and becomes a controlling element in civil society. . . . Without this society could not exist. With no right to the product of his labor no man would make a tool, or a garment, or build a shelter, or raise a crop. There could be no industry and no progress. It will be found too, historically, that the general well-being and progress of society has been in proportion to the freedom of every man to gain property in all legitimate ways, and to security in its possession. . . . The acquisition of property is required by love, because it is a powerful means of benefiting others. . . . A selfish getting of property, though better than a selfish indolence or wastefulness, is not to be encouraged. . . . Industry, frugality, carefulness, as ministering to a cheerful giving, would then not only be purged from all taint of meanness, but would be ennobled."[8] The essentials of the Hopkins position were three: individualism, the sanctity of private property, and the duty of stewardship.

The post-Appomattox evangelist of the refurbished Puritan doctrine of property was a Baptist minister of Philadelphia, Russell H. Conwell, whose popular lecture, *Acres of Diamonds*, was said to have been repeated throughout the East and Middle West six thousand times. Such popularity was evidence that Conwell's gospel harmonized with the mood of the American middle class. "To secure wealth is an honorable ambition, and is one great test of a person's usefulness to others," said the preacher over and over again. "Money is power. Every good man and woman ought to strive for power, to do good with it when obtained. Tens of thousands of men and women get

rich honestly. But they are often accused by an envious, lazy crowd of unsuccessful persons of being dishonest and oppressive. I say, Get rich, get rich! But get money honestly, or it will be a withering curse."[9] So was presented with forensic skill by Conwell the old doctrine of property and of stewardship. Its late nineteenth century version ran as follows: If God calls a man to make money in his earthly calling, he holds the wealth he acquires as the steward of the Lord. "The good Lord gave me my money," said that faithful Baptist, John D. Rockefeller, to the first graduating class of the university which he had founded, "and how could I withhold it from the University of Chicago?"[10] In 1900 Bishop Lawrence of Massachusetts rounded out and perfected the modernized formula. To acquire material wealth is natural and necessary, he argued. "In the long run, it is only to the man of morality that wealth comes. We believe in the harmony of God's Universe. We know that it is only by working along His laws natural and spiritual that we can work with efficiency. Only by working along the lines of right thinking and right living can the secrets and wealth of nature be revealed. . . . Godliness is in league with riches. . . . Material prosperity is helping to make the national character sweeter, more joyous, more unselfish, more Christlike. That is my answer to the question as to the relation of material prosperity to morality."[11] Bishop Lawrence had transformed Cotton Mather's row boat into an ocean liner.

[8] Mark Hopkins, *The Law of Love and Love as Law*, 1868, 182–183.

[9] Russell H. Conwell, *Acres of Diamonds*, 1890, 19. Quoted with the permission of Harper & Brothers.

[10] Quoted in John T. Flynn, *God's Gold*, 306. Quoted with the permission of Harcourt, Brace & Company.

[11] *World's Work*, I, 286–290.

Such was the Christian form of the late nineteenth century gospel of wealth. Its secular counterpart differed from it only in the dropping of the supernaturalistic trappings. This version received its most cogent expression in the writings of Andrew Carnegie, who did not share the illiteracy of some of his contemporary industrial chieftains. . . .[12]

The gospel of wealth perforce included an explanation of poverty, for in the Gilded Age the slum was as conspicuous as the millionaire. Both the Christian and the secular version of the formula developed against the background of blighted urban areas. The ecclesiastical preachers of the faith had their explanation. Poverty, taught the Porters and the Conwells, springs from laziness, lack of thrift, vice, and sometimes misfortune. This was the traditional explanation of the Puritan code of worldly asceticism. Poverty in the world, added the preachers, is as inevitable as sin and is largely the result of it. "The poor ye have with you always," said the Founder. To the poor man should be given aid and charity. His sins should be pointed out to him; he should be converted to the Christian faith and his feet set on the road called Straight.

The explanation of poverty by the secular prophets of the gospel of wealth did not differ fundamentally from that of the divines. Out of his Shakespeare, Carnegie clipped his answer to the many protesters complaining that success was hard in 1890:

"The fault, dear Brutus, is not in our stars,
But in ourselves, that we are underlings."

He added: "Avenues greater in number, wider in extent, easier of access than ever before existed, stand open to the sober, frugal, energetic and able mechanic, to the scientifically educated youth, to the office boy and to the clerk — avenues through which they can reap greater successes than ever before within the reach of these classes in the history of the world. . . . The millionaires who are in active control started as poor boys, and were trained in that sternest but most efficient of all schools — poverty. . . . Congratulate poor young men upon being born to that ancient and honorable degree which renders it necessary that they should devote themselves to hard work."[13] Poverty, then, was viewed in terms of the individual, not of the mass. For the individual it was, or at least could be, a transient state. It was a blessing in disguise to the one who rose above it, but to him who did not, it was a symbol of shame, a sort of scarlet letter proclaiming that he was wanting in ability or character, or both.

The gospel of wealth was the intellectual concept of a generation that had stumbled upon easy money in a terrain well protected by nature from foreign brigands. It was the result produced when the individualism of a simpler agricultural and commercial civilization was carried over into a society luxuriating in all essential natural resources. But it was not the only result; this gospel of morality and of prosperity had its antithesis in the irresponsible philosophy of grab. The ill-fated gold corner of Fisk and Gould in 1867, the swindles of Crédit Mobilier, the wars between powerful bands of railroad buccaneers, the exploitation of the defenseless immigrant laborer, the sleight of hand which made valueless the bonds purchased with the

12 [There follows a summary of the article by Carnegie which is printed above, pp. 1 ff. — Ed.]

13 Andrew Carnegie, *The Empire of Business,* 1902, 18, 109, 122. Quoted with the permission of The Carnegie Foundation.

savings of the small investor, the stubborn and usually effective resistance of
great corporations to social legislation in
the states, and Mark Hanna's philosophy
of the public be damned, were also ide-
ological patterns produced by the same
situation which gave rise to Carnegie's
vision of a material paradise. They were
summed up in the philosophy of the
greatest of Republican bosses, Matthew
Stanley Quay. Asked, after he had ele-
vated himself to the Senate of the United
States, why he did not work for the
people, he is said to have affirmed that he
did. "I work for the men the people work
for." Jay Gould and Russell H. Conwell
represented the two extremes of individualism in an industrial age. When Conwell's thesis, to use the dialectic of Hegel
or of Marx, was set against Gould's antithesis, the synthesis was Daniel Drew,
master fleecer of the lambs and founder
of Drew Theological Seminary.

Was, then, the gospel of wealth merely
a sham? It was called such by the critics
of the new American overlords, and they
were able to document their charges with
distressing frequency. Had the gospel of
wealth been nothing but hypocrisy, however, it could scarcely have outlasted the
century. It was, in fact, not merely the
philosophy of a few rich men but a faith
which determined the thinking of millions of citizens engaged in small enterprises. Its basic emphasis was upon the
responsibility of the individual, confronting the hard uncertainty of life. The
gospel of wealth explained the meaning
of life with a metaphor that called life a
testing period in which those selected for
distinction must unite character with
ability, and magnanimity with power. It
was the philosophy which lay behind the
private charity for which the Americans
of the Gilded Age became justly famous.

It was an effort to carry the idealism and
the moral code of Christianity and of the
democratic faith into a rapidly developing capitalism. The gospel of wealth
sought to harmonize competitive acquisitiveness with the fundamental moral
law. Out of it came the unadvertised gift
to the needy family, the boys' club in a
poorer section of the city, the private
university, and the great foundation. It
was the first effort to make a complete
rationalization of capitalism, and it was
the capitalist's answer to his Marxist
critics.

But American capitalism in the last
three decades of the nineteenth century
was not on the defensive. It was triumphant. The depressions following the
panics of 1873 and of 1893 had destroyed
many individuals, but they had raised no
important doubts in the American mind.
In 1900 the sky was cloudless; the attacks
of labor in 1877, in 1886, and in 1894 had
come to naught, and the Bryan crusade
for inflation in 1896 had been turned
back. The gospel of wealth was the core
of a capitalistic philosophy for the individual and for society. It was a fighting
faith. Through this faith the American
business man said in effect:

We of the capitalistic persuasion put
trust in the individual man. We make him
a part, according to his particular skill,
of a great and far-reaching industrial organization. We demote him when his
ability fails, and discard him if we find
a serious flaw of character. In our system
there is nothing, save his own shortcomings, to prevent his rising from the
bottom to the top. We have, then, a
method, better than that of practical
politics, for selecting the leaders of a
democracy. By a process of pitiless testing we discover who are the strong, and
who are the weak. To the strong we give

power in the form of the autocratic control of industry and of wealth with which the leader, who has thus risen by a process of natural selection, can and does do for the masses of the community what they could never do for themselves. We agree with Alexander Hamilton that the voice of the able few should be equal to, nay, greater than that of the mediocre many in the actual government of society. So we demand that the political State shall leave us alone. We have little faith in the State as a constructive agency and less in it as an efficient instrument. The politician is a slave to the whims of the masses, a master of favoritism for his own ends, and a waster of the public substance. We demand of the State protection of property. For this purpose we ask an adequate police, a sound banking system, a sound currency based on gold, and court decisions to nullify social legislation confiscatory in character. We demand a tariff to protect us against our foreign competitors and a navy to guard our commerce and our stakes in other lands. When the State has fulfilled these, its proper functions, we ask it to leave us alone. We point to the progress already achieved under *laissez faire*. We guarantee that, if our conditions are met, the sun of prosperity will fill the land with light and happiness.

This faith and philosophy became the most persuasive siren in American life. It filled the highways with farm boys trekking to the city. It drained the towns and countryside of Europe. It persuaded the educated young man that the greatest rewards of life were to be found in the business world. It taught the ambitious that power lies in wealth rather than in political office. It penetrated the workshop and paralyzed the effort of the labor leader undertaking a crusade for justice to the working man. Who would choose to be a labor leader when, in expanding and developing America, he might become a captain of industry?

Inevitably the philosophy produced a prescription for achieving individual well-being. A corollary of the gospel of wealth was the popular formula of success. The stream of success literature which appeared after the Civil War became a flood by the end of the century. The patterns displayed in these writings suggest the intellectual climate in which the gospel of wealth flourished. "Young men," said Horace Greeley, "I would have you believe that success in life is within the reach of every one who will truly and nobly seek it." L. U. Reavis made this sentiment of the New York *Tribune's* editor the theme of a little volume which he brought out in 1871 and called *Thoughts for the Young Men of America, or a Few Practical Words of Advice to those Born in Poverty and Destined to be Reared in Orphanage.* Success, taught Reavis, depends upon a few simple rules: "Don't be Discouraged. Do the Best You Can. Be Honest, and Truthful and Industrious. Do Your Duty, and Live Right; Learn to Read, then Read all the Books and Newspapers You Can and All Will Be Well After Awhile."[14] In a thousand variations of phrase this simple prescription for success was presented to all Americans able to read the English language. It was as universal as those other panaceas, "Castoria" and the compound of Lydia Pinkham. It was acted out in the adventures and successes of heroes of novels by Horatio Alger and in the biographies for juveniles by William Makepeace

[14] L. U. Reavis, "Thoughts for the Young Men of America, etc.," enlarged ed., 1873, 11–12.

Thayer. In 1880 the latter paused to write *Tact, Push and Principle* because a friend had written to the author: "The delusions of the times ought to be exposed, and young men made to understand the *principle* wins, in the long run, instead of luck or unscrupulous scheming."[15] Thayer completed his exposé of the contemporary delusions in three hundred and fifty-four pages and concluded: "It is quite evident from the foregoing that religion requires the following very reasonable things of every young man, namely: that he should make the most of himself possible; that he should watch and improve his opportunities; that he should be industrious, upright, faithful, and prompt; that he should task his talents, whether one or ten, to the utmost; that he should waste neither time nor money; that *duty*, and not pleasure or ease, should be his watchword. And all this is precisely what we have seen to be demanded of all young men in reliable shops and stores. Religion uses all the just motives of worldly wisdom, and adds thereto those higher motives that immortality creates. Indeed, we might say that religion demands success."[16] In short, the theme song of the success broadcasters of post-Appomattox years was the old Puritan code of worldly asceticism. Possess the Puritan virtues and "failure is impossible. *Not* having them success is impossible."[17] "The top, in this little world," said another success philosopher, "is not so very high, and patient climbing will bring you to it ere you are aware."[18] The number and sales of the success books make clear that purveying the time-worn patent formula

was a profitable business. Its Christian phrases are evidence of the importance of religion on the intellectual climate of the 1870's and 1880's.

In the next decade, however, a significant change occurred in the success literature. The God of the Puritans faded gradually from the pages of the success books and was replaced by a strange and worldly mysticism called New Thought. Like Christian Science this new faith stemmed ultimately from the ideas of the Portland healer, Phineas P. Quimby. But New Thought lacked the peculiar variations of Mrs. Eddy on the basic theme of mental suggestion. In the New Thought version of the success formula, the old virtues were still important, but new words and phrases appeared: "personal magnetism"; "mental control"; "the subtle thought waves, or thought vibrations, projected from the human mind"; the "Law of Attraction"; and the "Law of Success." Use "the subtle thought waves," advised the prophets of the New Faith, and sell the prospect a bill of goods. It was the origin of "high pressure salesmanship." "The currents of knowledge, of wealth, of success, are as certain and fixed as the tides of the sea," wrote Orison Swett Marden in 1894 in his first book, *Pushing to the Front.* The law of prosperity, he concluded in 1922, "is just as definite as the law of gravitation, just as unerring as the principles of mathematics. It is a mental law. Only by thinking abundance can you realize the abundant prosperous life that is your birthright."[19] Marden's publishers sold more than three million copies of his books. Though he never formally united with the cult of New Thought, his writ-

---

[15] William Makepeace Thayer, *Tact, Push and Principle*, 1881, 8.

[16] *Ibid.*, 354.

[17] H. L. Reade, *Success in Business, or Money and How to Make It*, 1875, 66.

[18] J. G. Holland, *Every-Day Topics*, 1876, 112.

[19] Orison Swett Marden, *Prosperity, How to Attract It*, 1922, 4–5. For an excellent study of the American success cult see A. Whitney Griswold, unpublished thesis, Sterling Library, Yale University.

ings were filled with the ideas of the movement. The success philosophy was going naturalistic; by the development of a pseudo-psychology it was becoming "scientific." This change in the pattern of the literature of success was evidence which suggested that Carnegie's naturalistic version of the larger gospel of wealth was triumphing over the supernaturalism of Hopkins and of Conwell.

The supplanting of the phrases of religion by the catch words of New Thought in the jargon of the success literature suggests also a decline in the influence and prestige of Protestantism as the nineteenth century closed. Evidence to be brought out later makes clear that Christianity lost in the post-Appomattox decades its old authoritative position in American society. "Science" became the god of the new day. The developing technology which made possible the new industrialism was founded upon a workshop materialism; and empiricism guided the development of the new corporations. Before the Civil War, the Protestant churches had sought breathlessly to make their expansion keep pace with the swiftly moving frontier. After that disaster they were confronted by cities ballooning into monster population centers. Their task of adjustment was immediate and urgent.

For post-Civil War American Protestantism, the gospel of wealth became a formula which permitted the Church to make peace with popular materialism. The ancient tendency in the Christian religion to withdraw from the world, to stress the warfare between the spirit and the flesh, to think in terms of other-worldliness, was checked in rich America after the Civil War. In that age men emphasized the here and now. A people whose accumulation of wealth was rapidly increasing felt less need of the con-solation of a belief in a life to come. Spirituality does not normally flourish in a materialistic age. Protestantism, always sensitive to shifts in the mores, made quick adjustment to the trend of the times. The Christian version of the gospel as preached by Bishop Lawrence and by Russell H. Conwell was, in effect, a Protestant stratagem to retain for itself a place in the new social order, to provide itself with a function, in short, to save itself as a significant social institution. Urban Protestantism cultivated the middle and upper classes who possessed the ultimate power in American society.

It is true that there were revolters within the churches. These will be considered in another place. It is also true that there was a sincere minority who strove to play the rôle of steward of the Lord to the full extent of their ability. Russell H. Conwell, the founder of Temple University, was one of these. But for American Protestantism as a whole, the gospel of wealth as presented by Conwell and by Lawrence was a sign of decadence. When a species in nature approaches the end of its course, it frequently tends to exaggerate the weapons or the armament which established its position. So, in time, the tusks of the sabre-toothed tiger grew too long, and those of the mastodon curved until they were no longer useful. As the end of the nineteenth century approached, American cities saw a spinescent Protestantism converting its substance into costly and extravagant edifices, material symbols of the ecclesiastical gospel of wealth. A similar phenomenon among the Catholics came later.

The gospel of wealth of the Gilded Age, later dubbed "rugged individualism," grew out of changed social conditions which, in turn, had been brought about by the rise of industrial capitalism.

The formulation of its doctrines depended heavily, in the early post-Appomattox years, upon current religious thinking. As the prestige of orthodox Protestantism declined because of the growing importance of science in popular thought, the formulas of the gospel of wealth were expressed more and more frequently in secular language. Yet, in spite of the shifts in phraseology, the essentials of the gospel of wealth remained virtually unchanged throughout the last third of the century.

The core of the pattern was the doctrine of the free individual with emphasis upon freedom of action in the economic sphere. The doctrine as it finally emerged was indebted to four different formulations of the philosophy of individualism. It derived, in the religious version of the gospel of wealth, from the Christian concept of the freedom of the individual as a moral agent. It contained the popular philosophy that life is a race in which the prizes should go to the swiftest of foot. In its economic implications the doctrine of the rugged individualists stemmed from the classical theories of Adam Smith and James Mill. This *laissez-faire* position was supported toward the end of the century, when the prestige of Darwinism was high, by the evolutionary concept of the struggle for existence. The persistent American philosophy of individualism never had greater intellectual support than in the last two decades of the nineteenth century.

The gospel of wealth was not a fully developed social philosophy. Yet it contained implications which caused it to range far in the field of social thought. Summary enumeration of these assists in achieving an understanding of the power of this pattern in popular American thinking.

The gospel of wealth implied that the government of society in that most important of all areas, the economic, should be in the hands of a natural aristocracy. This leadership should be chosen in the hard school of competition. The rugged individualists assumed that the competitive struggle of the market selects out the weak and the incompetent and puts in positions of power those individuals who are distinguished for initiative, vision, judgment, and organizing ability. The prophets of the gospel of wealth believed that the best interests of society are furthered by putting the government of the economic area of society into the hands of these natural leaders. This ideal, of course, became the fact. Industries became economic autocracies. Management was supreme within the boundaries of its particular economic domain. The sanction behind management was the possession of economic power.

The corollary to the doctrine of a natural leadership was the philosophy of the police function of the State. The State exists, taught Porter, McCosh, and Carnegie, to maintain order and to protect property. Its activities must be limited to these functions. In order to function as a policeman the State must possess power. Possession of authority, however, tends to the desire on the part of officials to increase their control. Such increase naturally leads to attempts on the part of the State to interfere with the arrangements of the economic government set up by the natural leaders within particular industrial bailiwicks. Under such circumstances the State may become malevolent. Individuals must protect themselves. For purposes of protection bills of rights were incorporated in the early state constitutions as well as in the instrument which established the federal government.

One of the chief reasons why the meddling State is dangerous to society, the argument continued, is to be found in the fact that the usages and institutions of political democracy do not put men of ability into positions of power. Politics lifts mediocrity into the saddle. The evil connotations of the words, "politics" and "politician," were evidence of the popular judgment concerning the defects of realistic democracy. The gospel of wealth was a philosophy which functioned as a defense of economic government in the hands of what was supposed to be a natural aristocracy of ability against political government in the hands of mediocrity.

The prophets of the gospel of wealth assumed that the doctrine of stewardship established a proper and adequate control over the government of the economic leaders. Carnegie emphasized that stewardship would tie together a society which was dividing into classes. The more able, and hence the more wealthy, would dedicate their superior talents to the task of doing for the less able what they could not do for themselves. Through such a paternalistic pattern the class divisions would be overcome and the poor and the rich united.

The gospel of wealth inevitably implied a philosophy of poverty. Poverty should be for the individual a temporary status. With initiative, industry, and ability he should rise above it. For the masses who do not rise, poverty must be a badge of failure proclaiming that the individual is defective in capacity or morals or both. The philosophy emphasized individual responsibility. It implied that the democratic doctrine of the free individual has no meaning, if the individual citizen is not willing to buy his liberty at the price of responsibility.

The gospel of wealth assumed that the poor, the less fortunate in the competition of the market, would accept the leadership of the men who, rising to the top, became the industrial barons of the day. In making this assumption the proponents of the formula ignored two possibilities. The first was that those who failed in the economic struggle of the market might attempt to recoup their fortunes by an appeal to politics, that they might seek to win by political action what they had failed to get by economic action. The other possibility was that the underlings might raise up leaders out of their own number, acquire power by organization, and challenge the autocracy of industrial government. The last decade of the century saw both these possibilities become realities. Then the gospel of wealth became primarily a defense formula for the maintenance of the economic and social *status quo*.

The Right Reverend William Lawrence:

THE RELATION OF WEALTH TO MORALS

THERE is a certain distrust on the part of our people as to the effect of material prosperity on their morality. We shrink with some foreboding at the great increase of riches, and question whether in the long run material prosperity does not tend toward the disintegration of character.

History seems to support us in our distrust. Visions arise of their fall from splendor of Tyre and Sidon, Babylon, Rome, and Venice, and of great nations too. The question is started whether England is not to-day, in the pride of her wealth and power, sowing the wind from which in time she will reap the whirlwind.

Experience seems to add its support. Is it not from the ranks of the poor that the leaders of the people have always risen? Recall Abraham Lincoln and patriots of every generation.

The Bible has sustained the same note. Were ever stronger words of warning uttered against the deceitfulness of riches than those spoken by the peasant Jesus, who Himself had no place to lay His head? And the Church has through the centuries upheld poverty as one of the surest paths to Heaven: it has been a mark of the saint.

To be sure, in spite of history, experience, and the Bible, men have gone on their way making money and hailing with joy each age of material prosperity. The answer is: "This only proves the case; men are of the world, riches are deceitful, and the Bible is true; the world is given over to Mammon. In the increase of material wealth and the accumulation of riches the man who seeks the higher life has no part."

In the face of this comes the statement of the chief statistician of our census — from one, therefore, who speaks with authority: "The present census, when completed, will unquestionably show that the visible material wealth in this country now has a value of ninety billion dollars. This is an addition since 1890 of twenty-five billion dollars. This is a saving greater than all the people of the Western Continent had been able to make from the discovery of Columbus to the breaking out of the Civil War."

If our reasoning from history, experience, and the Bible is correct, we, a Christian people, have rubbed a sponge over the pages of the Bible and are in for orgies and a downfall to which the fall of Rome is a very tame incident.

May it not be well, however, to revise our inferences from history, experience, and the Bible? History tells us that, while riches have been an item and an indirect cause of national decay, innumerable other conditions entered in. Therefore, while wealth has been a source of danger, it has not necessarily led to demoralization.

That leaders have sprung from the ranks of the poor is true and always

From the *World's Work*, 1 (January, 1901), 286–292. Reprinted by permission.

will be true, so long as force of character exists in every class. But there are other conditions than a lack of wealth at the source of their uprising.

And as to the Bible: — while every word that can be quoted against the rich is as true as any other word, other words and deeds are as true; and the parables of our Lord on the stewardship of wealth, His association with the wealthy, strike another and complementary note. Both notes are essential to the harmony of His life and teachings. His thought was not of the conditions, rich or poor, but of a higher life, the character rising out of the conditions — fortunately, for we are released from that subtle hypocrisy which has beset the Christian through the ages, bemoaning the deceitfulness of riches and, at the same time, working with all his might to earn a competence, and a fortune if he can.

Man "Born to Be Rich"

Now we are in a position to affirm that neither history, experience, nor the Bible necessarily sustains the common distrust of the effect of material wealth on morality. Our path of study is made more clear. Two positive principles lead us out on our path.

The first is that man, when he is strong, will conquer Nature, open up her resources, and harness them to his service. This is his play, his exercise, his divine mission.

"Man," says Emerson, "is born to be rich. He is thoroughly related, and is tempted out by his appetites and fancies to the conquest of this and that piece of Nature, until he finds his well-being in the use of the planet, and of more planets than his own. Wealth requires, besides the crust of bread and the roof, the freedom of the city, the freedom of the earth." "The strong race is strong on these terms."

Man draws to himself material wealth as surely, as naturally, and as necessarily as the oak draws the elements into itself from the earth.

The other principle is that, in the long run, it is only to the man of morality that wealth comes. We believe in the harmony of God's Universe. We know that it is only by working along His laws natural and spiritual that we can work with efficiency. Only by working along the lines of right thinking and right living can the secrets and wealth of Nature be revealed. We, like the Psalmist, occasionally see the wicked prosper, but only occasionally.

Put two men in adjoining fields, one man strong and normal, the other weak and listless. One picks up his spade, turns over the earth, and works till sunset. The other turns over a few clods, gets a drink from the spring, takes a nap, and loafs back to his work. In a few years one will be rich for his needs, and the other a pauper dependent on the first, and growling at his prosperity.

Put ten thousand immoral men to live and work in one fertile valley and ten thousand moral men to live and work in the next valley, and the question is soon answered as to who wins the material wealth. Godliness is in league with riches.

Now we return with an easier mind and clearer conscience to the problem of our twenty-five billion dollars in a decade.

My question is: Is the material prosperity of this Nation favorable or unfavorable to the morality of the people?

The first thought is, Who has prospered? Who has got the money?

I take it that the loudest answer would be, "The millionaires, the capitalists, and the incompetent but luxurious rich"; and, as we think of that twenty-five billion, our thoughts run over the yachts, the palaces, and the luxuries that flaunt themselves before the public.

Who the Rich Are

As I was beginning to write this paper an Irishman with his horse and wagon drew up at my back door. Note that I say *his* horse and wagon. Twenty years ago that Irishman, then hardly twenty years old, landed in Boston, illiterate, uncouth, scarcely able to make himself understood in English. There was no symptom of brains, alertness, or ambition. He got a job to tend a few cows. Soon the American atmosphere began to take hold. He discovered that here every man has his chance. With his first earnings he bought a suit of clothes; he gained self-respect. Then he sent money home; then he got a job to drive a horse; he opened an account at the savings bank; then evening school; more money in the bank. He changed to a better job, married a thrifty wife, and to-day he owns his house, stable, horse, wagon, and bicycle; has a good sum at the bank, supports five children, and has half a dozen men working under him. He is a capitalist, and his yearly earnings represent the income on $30,000. He had no "pull"; he has made his own way by grit, physical strength, and increasing intelligence. He has had material prosperity. His older brother, who paid his passage over, has had material prosperity, and his younger brother, whose passage my friend paid, has had material prosperity.

Now we are beginning to get an idea as to where the savings are. They are in the hands of hundreds of thousands of just such men, and of scores of thousands of men whose incomes ten years ago were two and five thousand, and are now five and ten thousand; and of thousands of others whose incomes have risen from ten to thirty thousand. So that, when you

get to the multi-millionaires, you have only a fraction to distribute among them. And of them the fact is that only a small fraction of their income can be spent upon their own pleasure and luxury; the bulk of what they get has to be reinvested, and becomes the means whereby thousands earn their wages. They are simply trustees of a fraction of the national property.

When, then, the question is asked, "Is the material prosperity of this nation favorable or unfavorable to the morality of the people?" I say with all emphasis, "In the long run, and by all means, favorable!"

In other words, to seek for and earn wealth is a sign of a natural, vigorous, and strong character. Wherever strong men are, there they will turn into the activities of life. In the ages of chivalry you will find them on the crusades or seeking the Golden Fleece; in college life you will find them high in rank, in the boat, or on the athletic field; in an industrial age you will find them eager, straining every nerve in the development of the great industries. The race is to the strong. The search for material wealth is therefore as natural and necessary to the man as is the pushing out of its roots for more moisture and food to the oak. This is man's play, his exercise, the expression of his powers, his personality. You can no more suppress it than you can suppress the tide of the ocean. For one man who seeks money for its own sake there are ten who seek it for the satisfaction of the seeking, the power there is in it, and the use they can make of it. There is the exhilaration of feeling one's self grow in one's surroundings; the man reaches out, lays hold of this, that, and the other interest, scheme, and problem. He is building up a fortune? Yes, but his joy is also that he is building up a stronger, abler, and more powerful man. There are two men that have none of this ambition: the gilded, listless youth and the ragged listless pauper to whom he tosses a dime; they are in the same class.

We are now ready to take up the subject in a little more detail. How is it favorable? The parable of my Irish friend gives the answer.

In the first place, and as I have already suggested, the effort to make his living and add to his comforts and power gives free play to a man's activities and leads to a development of his faculties. In an age and country where the greater openings are in commercial lines, there the stronger men and the mass of them will move. It is not a question of worldliness or of love of money, but of the natural use and legitimate play of men's faculties. An effort to suppress this action is not a religious duty, but a disastrous error, sure to fail.

Self-Respect and Self-Mastery

Besides this natural play of the faculties comes the development of self-respect and ambition. In the uprise from a lower to a higher civilization, these are the basal elements. Watch the cart-loads of Polish or Italian immigrants as they are hauled away from the dock. Study their lifeless expression, their hang-dog look, and their almost cowering posture. Follow them and study them five years later: note the gradual straightening of the body, the kindling of the eye, and the alertness of the whole person as the men, women, and children begin to realize their opportunities, bring in their wages, and move to better quarters. Petty temptations and deep degradations that might have overwhelmed them on their arrival cannot now touch them.

With this comes also the power of self-mastery. The savage eats what he kills and spends what he has. In the movement towards civilization through material wealth, questions come up for decision every hour. Shall I spend? Shall I save? How shall I spend? How can I earn more? Shall I go into partnership with a capital of ten dollars, or shall I wait until I have fifty dollars?

Wage earners are not to-day, as they were in earlier days, hungering for the bare physical necessities of life. They are hungering now, and it marks an upward movement in civilization, for higher things, education, social life, relaxation, and the development of the higher faculties.

To be sure, a certain fraction wilt under the strain, take to drink, to lust, to laziness. There is always the thin line of stragglers behind every army, but the great body of the American people are marching upwards in prosperity through the mastery of their lower tastes and passions to the development of the higher. From rags to clothes, from filth to cleanliness, and from disease to health; from bare walls to pictures; from ignorance to education; from narrow and petty talk to books and music and art; from superstition to a more rational religion; from crudity to refinement; from self-centralization to the conception of a social unity.

Here in this last phrase we strike the next step in development. In this increase of wealth, this rapid communication which goes with it, this shrinking of the earth's surface and unifying of peoples through commerce, men and women are realizing their relations to society.

That there are those who in the deepest poverty sustain the spirit of unselfishness and exhibit a self-sacrifice for others which puts their richer neighbors to the blush we know by experience. At the same time, the fact is that for the mass and in the long run grinding poverty does grind down the character: in the struggle for bare existence and for the very life of one's children there is developed an intense self-centralization and a hardness which is destructive of the social instinct and of the finer graces. When, however, through the increase of wealth man has extended his interests, his vision, and his opportunities, "he is thoroughly related." His lines run out in every direction; he lays his finger upon all the broader interests of life, the school, the church, and the college. He reaches through commerce to the ends of the earth. He discovers one bond which is essential to the social unity in this commercial age — the bond of faith in other men; for in credit, on belief in others, our whole social and commercial fabric is built. And when a man has reached this point, he has indeed reached one of the high plateaus of character: from this rise the higher mountain peaks of Christian graces, but here he is on the standing-ground of the higher civilization.

As I write I can almost feel the silent protest of some critics. Are not these qualities, self-respect, self-mastery, a sense of social unity, and mutual confidence, the commonplaces of life? Is this the only response of material wealth in its relation to morality?

These are to us now the commonplaces of life: they are at the same time the fundamentals of character and of morality. If material prosperity has been one of the great instruments (and I believe it has) in bringing the great body of our people even to approach this plateau of character, it has more than justified itself.

One might, however, mention other and finer qualities that follow in these days the train of prosperity. I instance only one. We will strike up one mountain peak: it is that of joyful and grateful service.

The Privilege of Grateful Service

In other days we have heard much of "the sweet uses of adversity": the note still lingers in sermons and will linger as long as Christianity stands. There is, however, the other note that sounds strong in these days, — the privilege of grateful service.

I have in mind now a man of wealth (you can conjure up many like him) who lives handsomely and entertains; he has everything that purveys to his health and comfort. All these things are tributary to what? To the man's efficiency in his complete devotion to the social, educational, and charitable interests to which he gives his life. He is Christ's as much as was St. Paul, he is consecrated as was St. Francis of Assissi; and in recognition of the bounty with which God has blessed him he does not sell all that he has, but he uses all that he has, and, as he believes, in the wisest way, for the relief of the poor, the upbuilding of social standards, and the upholding of righteousness among the people. The Christian centuries, with all their asceticism and monasticism, with their great and noble saints, have, I believe, never witnessed a sweeter, more gracious, and more complete consecration than that which exists in the lives of hundreds of men and women in the cities and towns of this country, who, out of a sense of grateful service to God for His bounty, are giving themselves with all joy to the welfare of the people. And if ever Christ's words have been obeyed to the letter, they are obeyed to-day by those who are living out His precepts of the stewardship of wealth.

As we think of the voluntary and glad service given to society, to the State, the Church, to education, art, and charity, of the army of able men and women who, without thought of pay, are serving upon directories of savings banks and national banks, life insurance companies, railroads, mills, trusts and corporations, public commissions, and offices of all sorts, schools and colleges, churches and charities; as we run our thoughts over the free services of the doctors, of the lawyers, for their poorer clients, we are amazed at the magnitude of unpaid service, which is now taken for granted, and at the cheerful and glad spirit in which it is carried through. Material prosperity is helping to make the national character sweeter, more joyous, more unselfish, more Christlike. That is my answer to the question as to the relation of material prosperity to morality.

Again I feel a silent protest. Is not the writer going rather far? We did not believe that our twenty-five billions would lead to orgies; but is he not getting rather close to the millennium? Are there no shadows and dark spaces in the radiance which he seems to think that wealth is shedding around us?

Yet, my friendly critic, there are, and to a mention of a few of them I give the pages that are left.

The Spirit of Commercialism

First and most pervasive, I name the spirit of commercialism. It crops up in many forms and places, hydra-headed.

Is it any wonder? When one realizes that in the last ten years seventy millions of people have earned their living, paid their bills, and have at the same time increased the property of the Nation by twenty-five billions of dollars, we reach a slight conception of the intensity, the industry, the enterprise, and the ability

with which those people have thought, worked, and reaped. One wonders that religion, charity, or culture have survived the strain at all. When the eye and ambition of a strong man are set upon a purpose, he sometimes neglects other considerations; he is not over nice about the rights of others; he occasionally overrides the weak, crushes out the helpless, and forgets to stop and pick up those that have fallen by the way.

We know how that was in England: we remember the report of the Commission by Lord Shaftesbury as to the horrible condition of the miners, men, women, and children. That was simply one phase in the development of the great movement of modern industrialism. It was a neglect and forgetfulness under a new pressure, rather than deliberate cruelty. The facts once known, attention called, — and reforms began; and they have been going on in behalf of the working people ever since. Much, very much, has been done.

As conditions change, much remains to do. The better adjustment of rights, wages, and taxes will call for the highest intelligence and strongest character. Again, the small tradesman has driven away the little counter where a widow earned her living, the larger tradesman has wiped out the small tradesman, and the department store is now finishing off some of the large tradesmen. It is hard, but it is a part of the great economic movement. It endangers some of the fundamentals of morality, and destroys for the time some of the finer graces.

Ephemeral success sometimes follows deceit, and that breeds a body of commercial frauds; but they cannot endure. A fortune is won by an unscrupulous adventurer; and a hundred fortunes are lost and characters spoiled in trying to follow suit. An ignorant man happens upon wealth or by some mysterious commercial ability wins wealth, and he then thinks himself omniscient. He, not God, is his own creator. He goes to church, but he is Godless. When a nation of people have been seeking for clothes, houses, and comforts in the upbuilding of civilization, is it any wonder that they do not realize that a man's life consisteth not in the abundance of things that he possesseth? There are deceit, hardness, materialism, and vulgarity in the commercial world; and to me the vulgarest of all is not the diamond-studded operator, but the horde of mothers crushing each other around the bargain counter in their endeavor to get something, and that so small, for nothing. The worst of commercialism is that it does not stop at the office, but enters the home, taints the marriage vow, and poisons social life at its springs.

Beyond these rudimentary forms of commercialism, there is another, even more dangerous, because it threatens the liberties and rights of the people. The eye of the public is on it now. I refer to the relation of concentrated masses of wealth to the public service.

I have no time to more than suggest a few of the conditions that have led up to this. Industrial enterprise has drawn many of the strongest and ablest men from political to commercial interests; society and legislation now do for the people what in other days the landlord did; they are concerned more and more with industrial, commercial, and financial questions, from the national tariff to the size of a house-drain. Just at this time, and because of our great industrial development and prosperity, a horde of ignorant voters waiting to be moulded by any strong leader have come to this shore. The wide distribution of wealth has driven merchants and mechanics,

widows and trustees of orphans, doctors and ministers, to invest their savings in great enterprises, corporations, and trusts, which, to succeed, must be directed by a few men. We have therefore this situation: a few men responsible for the safekeeping and development of enormous properties, dependent upon legislation, and a great mass of voters, many of them ignorant, represented by their own kind in city or state government, strongly organized by a leader who is in it for what he can get out of it, and who is ever alert with his legislative cohorts to "strike" the great corporations. The people believe that the officers of great corporations so manage that they can get what they want, call it by assessment, bribery, ransom, or what you will, and they brand those otherwise respectable men as cowards and traitors to public liberty.

The Rich Man and the Burglar

A burglar breaks into your house, awakes you, and "strikes" you for $500 which is in your safe downstairs. You expostulate: he answers that he will burn your house. But your children, you cry, will they be safe? He does not know: he wants the money. But if you give it to him, he will try the same on other people. It is against all public duty for you to yield. Again, the threat that he will burn your house; and you, miserable, conscience-stricken that you are doing a cowardly thing, and one against the safety of the public, crawl downstairs, open the safe, and hand over the cash. You have saved your house and children, but how about your duty to the public and your neighbors, as well as to yourself?

This is very much the position of the great trustees of capital, the heads of our great corporations, at the hands of the modern bandit. Shall they jeopardize the income of women and children, merchants and mechanics, and perhaps drive them into poverty? Or shall they accept the situation, yield to the threat, and trust to the authorities to seize the robber, or through an aroused public opinion so to vote, act, and legislate as to change the law and stop this modern brigandage? That some of the promoters and managers of great corporations are unscrupulous is undoubtedly true. The jail is none too good for them, if only the law would touch them. Nor have we 'a word of apology or justification for any man who yields to or encourages blackmail. The difficulty, however, is not a simple one. It concerns more than the directors and the politicians; it relates to the rights and liberties of the people. I do not have so much fear of the rich man in office, as I do of the poor but weak man in office and the rich man outside. Through the interplay of aroused public opinion, better legislation, and intelligent action, the relief will come. A younger generation, with its eye keen upon that danger-point, is coming to the front.

In some cities of China the houses have no windows on the street, only bare walls and the little door. The families are isolated, narrow, and selfish: there is no public spirit. When the Chinese boy returns home from his Christian Mission School, touched with the spirit of Christian civilization, his first work in bringing civilization to his home is to take a crowbar, knock a hole in the front wall, and make a window, that he may see out and the people see in. He unifies society and creates a public opinion. What is needed as our next step in civilization is to break a hole and make a window that the public may see into the great corporations and trusts and, what is just as important, that the managers may see out and recognize the sentiment of the public.

Light and action — heroic action! There are men to-day waiting and wanting to act, to throw off the shackles of the modern bandit; but they dare not alone: their trusts are too great. What is wanted is a group of men, high in position, great in power, who at great cost, if need be, will stand and say, "Thus far, up to the lines of the nicest honor, shalt thou go, and no farther."

The people have their eye upon the public service. An administration may pay political debts by pushing ignorant and unworthy men into the lower offices, but when it comes to filling positions of great responsibility the President could not, and would not if he could, appoint men less worthy than Wood in Cuba, Allen in Porto Rico, and Taft in the Philippines, men of force, intelligence, and character. Collegiate education does not insure character, but it does sift men and insure intelligence; and, as President Pritchett of the Massachusetts Institute of Technology pointed out in his inaugural address, though less than one per cent of our population are college men, yet from this very small fraction a majority of the legislative, executive, and judicial places of the General Government which have to do in any large way with shaping the policy and determining the character of the government, are chosen.

The Danger from Luxury

One other dark shadow, and I am done. The persistent companion of riches, — luxury and an ability to have what you want. That vice and license are rampant in certain quarters is clear; that vulgar wealth flaunts itself in the face of the people is beyond question; and that the people are rather amused at the spectacle must be confessed. The theatre syndicate will turn on to the boards whatever the people want; and the general tone of the plays speaks not well for the taste and morality of the people. The strain of temptation overwhelms a fraction of our youth. But one has no more right to test the result of prosperity by the small class of the lazy and luxurious than he has to test the result of poverty by the lazy tramp.

With all this said, the great mass of the people are self-restrained and simple. Material prosperity has come apace, and on the whole it uplifts. Responsibility sobers men and nations. We have learned how to win wealth: we are learning how to use and spend it. Every year marks a long step in advance in material prosperity, and character must march in step. Without wealth, character is liable to narrow and harden. Without character, wealth will destroy. Wealth is upon us, increasing wealth. The call of to-day is, then, for the uplift of character, — the support of industry, education, art, and every means of culture; the encourage-ment of the higher life; and, above all, the deepening of the religious faith of the people; the rekindling of the spirit, that, clothed with her material forces, the great personality of this Nation may fulfil her divine destiny.

I have been clear, I trust, in my opinion that material prosperity is in the long run favorable to morality. Let me be as clear in the statement of that eternal truth, that neither a man's nor a nation's life consists in the abundance of things that he possesseth.

In the investment of wealth in honest enterprise and business, lies our path of character. In the investment of wealth in all that goes towards the uplift of the people in education, art, and religion is another path of character. Above all, and first of all, stands the personal life. The immoral rich man is a traitor to himself, to his material as well as spiritual interests. Material prosperity is upon us; it is marching with us. Character must keep step, ay, character must lead. We want great riches; we want also great men.

John Bates Clark:

THE SOCIETY OF THE FUTURE

IF the goal toward which progress is tending is not socialism, what is it? It must be good or we shall not believe that we are moving toward it. Optimism is the faith of healthy humanity. Without making assertions as to anything that is very remote, we may say that certain changes are undoubtedly going on; that they are taking us in a certain direction and toward a nearer goal that we can define. We shall reach it if economic laws continue to work and the general course of events continues unchanged.

The term "goal," indeed, scarcely describes what is thus before us; for it designates a stopping-place, whereas what is before us is a perpetual movement. The halting place of yesterday is the starting-point of to-day, and that of to-day is to be the starting-point of to-morrow. The state that we shall reach in two or three centuries may contain within itself all the gains that we can now easily imagine; but it will only be the beginning of acquisitions that are beyond the range of our present imaginings. It is easier to define intermediate states. What will society be after fifty years shall have passed and toward what state will it then be tending? To such a question as this economic movements afford a fairly confident answer.

In the first place, competition will survive. Trusts will not destroy it, and it may even become more effective than it

has been. The race for the profits that are to be gained by invention, by chemical discovery and by business organization will make the work of the world so efficient that its present power of production, great as it is, will, in the retrospect, seem like rude first steps in material civilization. We shall improve agriculture and get our living more easily; but we shall make larger gains in producing comforts and luxuries. More and more readily will the earth yield raw materials, and more easily will industry fashion them into fine commodities. We shall surround ourselves with a profusion of useful things, and so small will be the labor that many of them will cost that it will seem as if genii had a hand in bringing them to us. Machines will become more deft, powerful, rapid and automatic. They will get their motive power from cheap and abundant sources, and there will be little left for the workers who use them except to touch the buttons that set them moving. Dwellings and furnishings will improve, and vehicles will multiply till the amount of labor that is now the equivalent of a nickel will give a poor man a longer and more interesting drive than a costly equipage now gives a rich man. It may be that the wages of a day will take him to the mountains, and those of a hundred days will carry him through a European tour. With the powers in his hands which me-

From *The Independent,* 53 (July 18, 1901), 1649–1651.

chanical invention will confer the typical laborer will, in due time, attain the scale of substantial comfort on which well-to-do classes are now living.

If this is to be the fact, however, it is necessary not only that an abundance of products should be created, but that they should be created by and for the workers themselves. The distribution of wealth must be as satisfactory as the production of it is fruitful. It will be so if progress makes labor itself, and not merely industries in which labor is one agent, more and more productive. The empty-handed worker of the future, when he offers himself to an employer for hire, will carry in his hands a potential product for sale, and this product must be larger than the one that the worker of the present tenders. Improvements in method and in organization will enable him to do this. When a man works with a long lever the general result is larger than it is when he has a short one; but the important thing is that *that part of the result which is due to labor alone* is greater. A man and a modern machine create a larger product than did a man and an old fashioned tool; but the essential fact is that what the man himself can claim as his own and actually get is larger than it was in the days of hand labor. When the world shall be filled, as it were, with "genii of the lamp," the man who can call them into action will be a more important factor than is the man of the present, and he can himself create more and get more than can the worker of to-day.

This means, however, that the struggles of classes that will go on will give them their fair portion of the rich results of industry. In the period that is coming massed forces are to contend with each other. Every occupation, as a whole, will contend with every other occupation:

each business will want a high price for its particular product, and can get it only by taxing all who buy the product. Within each business there will be a further struggle, and massed labor will contend with massed capital in the effort to adjust wages. In each line of production both labor and capital will strive to become monopolistic. Capital will try to drive other capital off from its field, and labor will try to drive off other labor. These attempts cannot fully accomplish their objects. Here and there consolidations of capital will have limited success, and will make the position of competing capital perilous. Here and there also labor will have the same partial success in guarding its field against the intrusion of competing labor. The effect will be to favor some union laborers at the expense of others, and to make the democracy of labor imperfect. Workers will be ranged in strata, representing gradations of well being; but there is nothing in this that will prevent them all from rising together. They may keep their relative positions and all move upward.

This again requires that the principle of monopoly should everywhere be held in check. The influences that obstruct competition are themselves to be controlled, and if natural tendencies have their way they will be so. When a trust exacts too much, competitors will appear, in spite of all perils that may threaten them. When laborers in any occupation exact too large a premium over ordinary wages, workers will force themselves into their territory in spite of all that can be done to stop them. The imperfections of competition will put some workers into favored classes, but the competition which survives will be dominant, and will bring gains to all classes.

That this may be true the State at least must be democratic. Government by the people must not be allowed to vanish, and those who are ruled must nominate, elect and control their rulers. If we keep the representative principle at all, as for convenience we must, it will have to be attended by an immense increase of actual self-government. I chance to believe that we are to have the referendum, or what amounts to the referendum, in municipal, State and federal affairs. The difficulties in the way of this are not trifling, but they weigh far less than the evils that are in store for us if we do not have it. At the bottom it is for the rescue of competitive industry that we need it. Very insidious is the power that massed capital knows how to use in controlling the so-called representatives of the people, who are often rather the conscienceless substitutes for the people in the work of ruling. Labor should be able to do better than to compete with wealth in this direction. It should have open and honest ways of influencing the acts of the Government.

But shall we not, in this political sphere, have too much democracy? Clearly not, and that for several reasons, the chief of which is that the *demos* that will rule will not be the typical one that we think of in connection with the history of democratic States. It will not be a proletariat, but will be a body of workmen, most of whom will have a large stake in the industrial order. Their savings will grow and make them conservative wherever the security of property is in question. Their wages will enable them to make accumulations, and the Government of the future must be efficient enough to give them safe investments. Land, under one or another form of title, now affords to laborers their principal medium of investment; and there is little doubt that, for laborers, it will continue to be a favorite form of property. The confiscation of rent will not be popular with the coming democracy. Bonds and, in the end, even stocks must also be made available for a similar purpose. If tunnels and canals are dug by means of public funds, the bonds which States will issue will be available as far as they will go; but the society of the future will fall far short of what it ought to be unless the securities of corporations can be safely owned even by the poorer classes.

The world of the near future will not be one with inequalities leveled out of it; and to any persons to whom inequality of possessions seems inherently evil, this world will not be satisfactory. It will present a condition of vast and ever growing inequality. With a democracy that depends on a likeness of material possessions it will have nothing in common. The rich will continually grow richer and the multi-millionaires will approach the billion-dollar standard; but the poor will be far from growing poorer. They will surely and not always slowly recede from the poverty line, and rise toward the present standard of wealth. As the typical rich man enlarges his holdings — as his fortune increases from one million dollars to ten, from ten to a hundred and from a hundred to a thousand — the typical laborer will increase his wages from one dollar a day to two, from two to four and from four to eight. Such gains will mean indefinitely more to him than any possible increase of capital can mean to the rich.

If an earthly Eden is to come through competition it will come not in spite of, but by means of an enormous increase of inequality of outward possessions; but this very change will bring with it a continual approach to equality of genuine comfort. The capitalist may become too rich to sleep, while the laborer becomes so relatively rich that he can live in comfort and rest in peace. Near to the line of maximum happiness may be the lives of the better paid workers.

The most alluring possibility concerning the democracy of the future lies in the diffusion of culture. The well paid worker may have any amount of it for himself and his children. No tendency of the present is more marked than that which is slowly obliterating the differences in education which formerly prevailed; and with higher pay and easier labor the worker can more and more avail himself of the new condition. Refinements, as well as comforts, are to be included in the list of cheap things that can be had as the reward of common labor.

There is a moral effect of progress that is even better. A fraternity of the highest type is among the gains that are well within sight, and unlike fortunes, so far from perverting it, will bring it to perfection. Brotherly feeling is a weak thing, indeed, if the condition of its existence is that men shall be equally well off. Communism does not develop the finer sort of brotherhood; but inequality may develop it, if the moral fiber of the race shall grow strong. When men can regard each other with respect and affection in spite of enormous differences of wealth there will be some virility in their fraternal feeling. Well within sight is such a condition. As the prizes of political leadership and of social and intellectual eminence shall fall even more often to the man of labor than to the man of mere capital it may be that very few persons will see in the change any vulgarization of State or society. The *demos* of the future will not win such prizes unless it continues to develop in intellect and character; and if it does so develop, this fact will give it a clear title to any outward prizes it may win. If out of the democracy that is defined by mere possessions there shall come an aristocracy of personal quality, the result will be the best that evolution can give or that imagination can picture.

William Graham Sumner:
THE CONCENTRATION OF WEALTH: ITS ECONOMIC JUSTIFICATION

THE concentration of wealth I understand to include the aggregation of wealth into large masses and its concentration under the control of a few. In this sense the concentration of wealth is indispensable to the successful execution of the tasks which devolve upon society in our time. Every task of society requires the employment of capital, and involves an economic problem in the form of the most expedient application of material means to ends. Two features most prominently distinguish the present age from all which have preceded it: first, the great scale on which all societal undertakings must be carried out; and second, the transcendent importance of competent management, that is, of the personal element in direction and control.

I speak of "societal undertakings" because it is important to notice that the prevalent modes and forms are not confined to industrial undertakings, but are universal in all the institutions and devices which have for their purpose the satisfaction of any wants of society. A modern church is a congeries of institutions which seeks to nourish good things and repress evil ones; it has buildings, apparatus, a store of supplies, a staff of employees, and a treasury. A modern church (parish) will soon be as complex a system of institutions as a mediaeval monastery was. Contrast such an establishment with the corresponding one of fifty years ago.

A university now needs an immense "concentration of wealth" for its outfit and work. It is as restricted in its work as the corresponding institution of fifty years ago was, although it may command twenty times as much capital and revenue. Furthermore, when we see that all these and other societal institutions pay far higher salaries to executive officers than to workers, we must recognize the fact that the element of personal executive ability is in command of the market, and that means that it is the element which decides success. To a correct understanding of our subject it is essential to recognize the concentration of wealth and control as a universal societal phenomenon, not merely as a matter of industrial power, or social sentiment, or political policy.

Stated in the concisest terms, the phenomenon is that of a more perfect integration of all societal functions. The concentration of power (wealth), more dominant control, intenser discipline, and stricter methods are but modes of securing more perfect integration. When we perceive this we see that the concentra-

From *Essays of William Graham Sumner*, ed. Albert G. Keller and Maurice R. Davie, copyright 1934 by the Yale University Press. Reprinted by permission of the Yale University Press.

tion of wealth is but one feature of a grand step in societal evolution.

Some may admit that the concentration of wealth is indispensable, but may desire to distinguish between joint-stock aggregations on the one side and individual fortunes on the other. This distinction is a product of the current social prejudice and is not valid. The predominance of the individual and personal element in control is seen in the tendency of all joint-stock enterprises to come under the control of very few persons. Every age is befooled by the notions which are in fashion in it. Our age is befooled by "democracy"; we hear arguments about the industrial organization which are deductions from democratic dogmas or which appeal to prejudice by using analogies drawn from democracy to affect sentiment about industrial relations. Industry may be republican; it never can be democratic, so long as men differ in productive power and in industrial virtue. In our time joint-stock companies, which are in form republican, are drifting over into oligarchies or monarchies because one or a few get greater efficiency of control and greater vigor of administration. They direct the enterprise in a way which produces more, or more economically. This is the purpose for which the organization exists and success in it outweighs everything else. We see the competent men refuse to join in the enterprise, unless they can control it, and we see the stockholders willingly put their property into the hands of those who are, as they think, competent to manage it successfully. The strongest and most effective organizations for industrial purposes which are formed nowadays are those of a few great capitalists, who have great personal confidence in each other and who can bring together adequate means for whatever they desire to do. Some

such nucleus of individuals controls all the great joint-stock companies.

It is obvious that "concentration of wealth" can never be anything but a relative term. Between 1820 and 1830 Stephen Girard was a proverb for great wealth; to-day a man equally rich would not be noticed in New York for his wealth. In 1848 John Jacob Astor stood alone in point of wealth; to-day a great number surpass him. A fortune of $300,-000 was then regarded as constituting wealth; it was taken as a minimum above which men were "rich." It is certain that before long some man will have a billion. It is impossible to criticize such a moving notion. The concentration of capital is also necessarily relative to the task to be performed; we wondered lately to see a corporation formed which had a capital of a billion. No one will wonder at such a corporation twenty-five years hence.

There seems to be a great readiness in the public mind to take alarm at these phenomena of growth — there might rather seem to be reason for public congratulation. We want to be provided with things abundantly and cheaply; that means that we want increased economic power. All these enterprises are efforts to satisfy that want, and they promise to do it. The public seems to turn especially to the politician to preserve it from the captain of industry; but when has anybody ever seen a politician who was a match for a captain of industry? One of the latest phenomena is a competition of the legislatures of several states for the profit of granting acts of incorporation; this competition consists, of course, in granting greater and greater powers and exacting less and less responsibility.

It is not my duty in this place to make a judicial statement of the good and ill of the facts I mention — I leave to others to suggest the limitations and safeguards which are required. It is enough to say here that of course all power is liable to abuse; if anybody is dreaming about a millennial state of society in which all energy will be free, yet fully controlled by paradisaic virtue, argument with him is vain. If we want results we must get control of adequate power, and we must learn to use it with safeguards. If we want to make tunnels, and to make them rapidly, we have to concentrate supplies of dynamite; danger results; we minimize it, but we never get rid of it. In late years our streets have been filled with power-driven cars and vehicles; the risk and danger of going on the streets has been very greatly increased; the danger is licensed by law, and it is inseparable from the satisfaction of our desire to move about rapidly. It is in this light that we should view the evils (if there are any) from the concentration of wealth. I do not say that "he who desires the end desires the means," because I do not believe that that dictum is true; but he who will not forego the end must be patient with the incidental ills which attend the means. It is ridiculous to attempt to reach the end while making war on the means. In matters of societal policy the problem always is to use the means and reach the end as well as possible under the conditions. It is proper to propose checks and safeguards, but an onslaught on the concentration of wealth is absurd and a recapitulation of its "dangers" is idle.

In fact, there is a true correlation between (a) the great productiveness of modern industry and the consequent rapid accumulation of capital from one period of production to another and (b) the larger and larger aggregations of capital which are required by modern industry from one period of production to another. We see that the movement is constantly accelerated, that its scope is all the time widening, and that the masses of material with which it deals are greater and greater. The dominant cause of all this is the application of steam and electricity to transportation, and the communication of intelligence — things which we boast about as great triumphs of the nineteenth century. They have made it possible to extend efficient control, from a given central point, over operations which may be carried on at a great number of widely separated points, and to keep up a close, direct, and intimate action and reaction between the central control and the distributed agents. That means that it has become possible for the organization to be extended in its scope and complexity, and at the same time intensified in its activity. Now whenever such a change in the societal organization becomes possible it also becomes *inevitable*, because there is economy in it. If we confine our attention to industrial undertakings (although states, churches, universities, and other associations and institutions are subject to the same force and sooner or later will have to obey it) we see that the highest degree of organization which is possible is the one that offers the maximum of profit; in it the economic advantage is greatest. There is therefore a gravitation toward this degree of organization. To make an artificial opposition to this tendency from political or alleged moral, or religious, or other motives would be to have no longer any real rule of action; it would amount to submission to the control of warring motives without any real standards or tests.

It is a consequence of the principle just stated that at every point in the history of civilization it has always been necessary to concentrate capital in amounts large relatively to existing facts.

In low civilization chiefs control what capital there is, and direct industry; they may be the full owners of all the wealth or only the representatives of a collective theory of ownership. This organization of industry was, at the time, the most efficient, and the tribes which had it prospered better than others. In the classical states with slavery and in the mediaeval states with serfdom, the great achievements which realized the utmost that the system was capable of were attained only where wealth was concentrated in productive enterprises in amounts, and under management, which were at the maximum of what the system and the possibilities of the time called for. If we could get rid of some of our notions about liberty and equality, and could lay aside this eighteenth century philosophy according to which human society is to be brought into a state of blessedness, we should get some insight into the might of the societal organization: what it does for us, and what it makes us do. Every day that passes brings us new phenomena of struggle and effort between parts of the societal organization. What do they all mean? They mean that all the individuals and groups are forced against each other in a ceaseless war of interests, by their selfish and mutual efforts to fulfill their career on earth within the conditions set for them by the state of the arts, the facts of the societal organization, and the current dogmas of world philosophy. As each must win his living, or his fortune, or keep his fortune, under these conditions, it is difficult to see what can be meant in the sphere of industrial or economic effort by a "free man." It is no wonder that we so often hear angry outcries about being "slaves" from persons who have had a little experience of the contrast between the current notions and the actual facts.

In fact, what we all need to do is to be taught by the facts in regard to the notions which we ought to adopt, instead of looking at the facts only in order to pass judgment on them and make up our minds how we will change them. If we are willing to be taught by the facts, then the phenomena of the concentration of wealth which we see about us will convince us that they are just what the situation calls for. They ought to be because they are, and because nothing else would serve the interests of society.

I am quite well aware that, in what I have said, I have not met the thoughts and feelings of people who are most troubled about the "concentration of wealth." I have tried to set forth the economic necessity for the concentration of wealth; and I maintain that this is the controlling consideration. Those who care most about the concentration of wealth are indifferent to this consideration; what strikes them most is the fact that there are some rich men. I will, therefore, try to show that this fact also is only another economic justification of the concentration of wealth.

I often see statements published, in which the objectors lay stress upon the great *inequalities* of fortune, and, having set forth the contrast between rich and poor, they rest their case. What law of nature, religion, ethics, or the state is violated by inequalities of fortune? The inequalities prove nothing. Others argue that great fortunes are won by privileges created by law and not by legitimate enterprise and ability. This statement is true, but it is entirely irrelevant; we have to discuss the concentration of wealth within the facts of the institutions, laws, usages, and customs which our ancestors have bequeathed to us and which we allow to stand. If it is proposed to change any of these parts of the societal order, that is a proper subject of discussion, but it is aside from the concentration of wealth. So long as tariffs, patents, etc., are part of the system in which we live, how can it be expected that people will not take advantage of them; what else are they for? As for franchises, a franchise is only an *x* until it has been developed. It never develops itself; it requires capital and skill to develop it. When the enterprise is in the full bloom of prosperity the objectors complain of it, as if the franchise, which never was anything but an empty place where something might be created, had been the completed enterprise. It is interesting to compare the exploitation of the telephone with that of the telegraph fifty years earlier. The latter was, in its day, a far more wonderful invention, but the time and labor required to render it generally available were far greater than what has been required for the telephone, and the fortunes which were won from the former were insignificant in comparison with those which have been won from the latter. Both the public and the promoters acted very differently in the two cases. In these later times promoters seize with avidity upon an enterprise which contains promise, and they push it with energy and ingenuity, while the public is receptive to "improvements"; hence the modern methods offer very great opportunities, and the rewards of those men who can "size up" a situation and develop its controlling elements with sagacity and good judgment, are very great. It is well that they are so, because these rewards stimulate to the utmost all the ambitious and able men, and they make it certain that great and useful inventions will not long remain unexploited as they did formerly. Here comes, then, a new reaction on the economic system; new energy is infused into it, with hope and confidence.

We could not spare it and keep up the air of contentment and enthusiastic cheerfulness which characterizes our society. No man can acquire a million without helping a million men to increase their little fortunes all the way down through all the social grades. In some points of view it is an error that we fix our attention so much upon the very rich and overlook the prosperous mass, but the compensating advantage is that the great successes stimulate emulation the most powerfully.

What matters it then that some millionaires are idle, or silly, or vulgar; that their ideas are sometimes futile and their plans grotesque, when they turn aside from money-making? How do they differ in this from any other class? The millionaires are a product of natural selection, acting on the whole body of men to pick out those who can meet the requirement of certain work to be done. In this respect they are just like the great statesmen, or scientific men, or military men. It is because they are thus selected that wealth — both their own and that intrusted to them — aggregates under their hands. Let one of them make a mistake and see how quickly the concentration gives way to dispersion. They may fairly be regarded as the naturally selected agents of society for certain work. They get high wages and live in luxury, but the bargain is a good one for society. There is the intensest competition for their place and occupation. This assures us that all who are competent for this function will be employed in it, so that the cost of it will be reduced to the lowest terms; and furthermore that the competitors will study the proper conduct to be observed in their occupation. This will bring discipline and the correction of arrogance and masterfulness.

Elbert Hubbard: A MESSAGE TO GARCIA

IN all this Cuban business there is one man stands out on the horizon of my memory like Mars at perihelion.

When war broke out between Spain and the United States, it was very necessary to communicate quickly with the leader of the Insurgents. Garcia was somewhere in the mountain fastnesses of Cuba — no one knew where. No mail nor telegraph message could reach him. The President must secure his co-operation, and quickly.

What to do!

Some one said to the President, "There's a fellow by the name of Rowan will find Garcia for you, if anybody can."

Rowan was sent for and given a letter to be delivered to Garcia. How "the fellow by the name of Rowan" took the letter, sealed it up in an oilskin pouch, strapped it over his heart, in four days landed by night off the coast of Cuba from an open boat, disappeared into the jungle and in three weeks came out on the other side of the Island, having traversed a hostile country on foot, and delivered his letter to Garcia, are things I have no special desire now to tell in detail.

The point I wish to make is this: McKinley gave Rowan a letter to be delivered to Garcia; Rowan took the letter and did not ask, "Where is he at?" By the Eternal! there is a man whose form should be cast in deathless bronze and the statue placed in every college of the land. It is not book-learning young men need, nor instruction about this and that, but a stiffening of the vertebrae which will cause them to be loyal to a trust, to act promptly, concentrate their energies: do the thing — "Carry a message to Garcia."

General Garcia is dead now, but there are other Garcias.

No man, who has endeavored to carry out an enterprise where many hands were needed, but has been well nigh appalled at times by the imbecility of the average man — the inability or unwillingness to concentrate on a thing and do it.

Slip-shod assistance, foolish inattention, dowdy indifference, and half-hearted work seem the rule; and no man succeeds, unless by hook or crook, or threat, he forces or bribes other men to assist him; or mayhap, God in His goodness performs a miracle, and sends him an Angel of Light for an assistant. You, reader, put this matter to a test: You are sitting now in your office — six clerks are within call. Summon any one and make this request: "Please look in the encyclopedia and make a brief memorandum for me concerning the life of Correggio."

Will the clerk quietly say, "Yes sir," and go do the task?

On your life he will not. He will look at you out of a fishy eye and ask one or more of the following questions:

Who was he?

Which encyclopedia?

Where is the encyclopedia?

Was I hired for that?

Don't you mean Bismarck?

What's the matter with Charlie doing it?

Is he dead?

Is there any hurry?

Shan't I bring you the book and let you look it up yourself?

What do you want to know for?

And I will lay you ten to one that after you have answered the questions, and explained how to find the information, and why you want it, the clerk will go off and get one of the other clerks to help him try to find Garcia — and then come back and tell you there is no such man. Of course I may lose my bet, but according to the Law of Average, I will not.

Now if you are wise you will not bother to explain to your "assistant" that Correggio is indexed under the C's, not in the K's, but you will smile sweetly and say, "Never mind," and go look it up yourself.

And this incapacity for independent action, this moral stupidity, this infirmity of the will, this unwillingness to cheerfully catch hold and lift, are the things that put pure Socialism so far into the future. If men will not act for themselves, what will they do when the benefit of their effort is for all?

A first-mate with knotted club seems necessary; and the dread of getting "the bounce" Saturday night, holds many a worker to his place.

Advertise for a stenographer, and nine out of ten who apply, can neither spell nor punctuate — and do not think it necessary to.

Can such a one write a letter to Garcia?

"You see that book-keeper," said the foreman to me in a large factory.

"Yes, what about him?"

"Well, he's a fine accountant, but if I'd send him up town on an errand, he might accomplish the errand all right, and on the other hand, might stop at four saloons on the way, and when he got to Main Street, would forget what he had been sent for."

Can such a man be entrusted to carry a message to Garcia?

We have recently been hearing much maudlin sympathy expressed for the "down-trodden denizen of the sweat-shop" and the "homeless wanderer searching for honest employment," and with it all often go many hard words for the men in power.

Nothing is said about the employer who grows old before his time in a vain attempt to get frowsy ne'er-do-wells to do intelligent work; and his long, patient striving with "help" that does nothing but loaf when his back is turned. In every store and factory there is a constant weeding-out process going on. The employer is constantly sending away "help" that have shown their incapacity to further the interests of the business, and others are being taken on. No matter how good times are, this sorting continues, only if times are hard and work is scarce, the sorting is done finer — but out and forever out, the incompetent and unworthy go. It is the survival of the fittest. Self-interest prompts every employer to keep the best — those who can carry a message to Garcia.

I know one man of really brilliant parts who has not the ability to manage a business of his own, and yet who is absolutely worthless to any one else, because he carries with him constantly the insane suspicion that his employer is oppressing, or intending to oppress him. He cannot give orders; and he will not receive them.

Should a message be given him to take to Garcia, his answer would probably be, "Take it yourself, and be damned!"

To-night this man walks the streets looking for work, the wind whistling through his thread-bare coat. No one who knows him dare employ him, for he is a regular fire-brand of discontent. He is impervious to reason, and the only thing that can impress him is the toe of a thick-soled No. 9 boot.

Of course I know that one so morally deformed is no less to be pitied than a physical cripple; but in our pitying, let us drop a tear, too, for the men who are striving to carry on a great enterprise, whose working hours are not limited by the whistle, and whose hair is fast turning white through the struggle to hold in line dowdy indifference, slip-shod imbecility, and the heartless ingratitude, which, but for their enterprise, would be both hungry and homeless.

Have I put the matter too strongly? Possibly I have; but when all the world has gone a-slumming I wish to speak a word of sympathy for the man who succeeds — the man who, against great odds, has directed the efforts of others, and having succeeded, finds there's nothing in it: nothing but bare board and clothes.

I have carried a dinner pail and worked for day's wages, and I have also been an employer of labor, and I know there is something to be said on both sides. There is no excellence, per se, in poverty; rags are no recommendation; and all employers are not rapacious and high-handed, any more than all poor men are virtuous.

My heart goes out to the man who does his work when the "boss" is away, as well as when he is at home. And the man who, when given a letter for Garcia, quietly takes the missive, without asking any idiotic questions, and with no lurking intention of chucking it into the nearest sewer, or of doing aught else but deliver it, never gets "laid off," nor has to go on a strike for higher wages. Civilization is one long anxious search for just such individuals. Anything such a man asks shall be granted; his kind is so rare that no employer can afford to let him go. He is wanted in every city, town and village — in every office, shop, store and factory. The world cries out for such: he is needed, and needly badly — the man who can carry a message to Garcia.

Charles S. Peirce: THE CENTURY OF GREED

THE nineteenth century is now fast sinking into the grave, and we all begin to review its doings and to think what character it is destined to bear as compared with other centuries in the minds of future historians. It will be called, I guess, the Economical Century; for political economy has more direct relations with all the branches of its activity than has any other science. Well, political economy has its formula of redemption, too. It is this: Intelligence in the service of greed ensures the justest prices, the fairest contracts, the most enlightened conduct of all the dealings between men, and leads to the *summum bonum*, food in plenty and perfect comfort. Food for whom? Why, for the greedy master of intelligence. I do not mean to say that this is one of the legitimate conclusions of political economy, the scientific character of which I fully acknowledge. But the study of doctrines, themselves true, will often temporarily encourage generalisations extremely false, as the study of physics has encouraged necessitarianism. What I say, then, is that the great attention paid to economical questions during our century has induced an exaggeration of the beneficial effects of greed and of the unfortunate results of sentiment, until there has resulted a philosophy which comes unwittingly to this, that greed is the great agent in the elevation of the human race and in the evolution of the universe.

I open a handbook of political economy, — the most typical and middling one I have at hand, — and there find some remarks of which I will here make a brief analysis. I omit qualifications, sops thrown to Cerberus, phrases to placate Christian prejudice, trappings which serve to hide from author and reader alike the ugly nakedness of the greed-god. But I have surveyed my position. The author enumerates "three motives to human action":

The love of self;
The love of a limited class having common interests and feelings with one's self;
The love of mankind at large.

Remark, at the outset, what obsequious title is bestowed on greed, — "the love of self." Love! The second motive *is* love. In place of "a limited class" put "certain persons," and you have a fair description. Taking "class" in the old-fashioned sense, a weak kind of love is described. In the sequel, there seems to be some haziness as to the delimitation of this motive. By the love of mankind at large, the author does not mean that deep, subconscious passion that is properly so called; but merely public-spirit, perhaps little more than a fidget about pushing ideas. The author proceeds to a comparative estimate of the worth of these motives. Greed, says he, but using, of course, another word, "is not so great an evil as

A portion of an article first printed under the title "Evolutionary Love" in *The Monist*, 3 (January, 1893), 176–200. This excerpt comprises pp. 178–182.

is commonly supposed. . . . Every man can promote his own interests a great deal more effectively than he can promote any one else's, or than any one else can promote his." Besides, as he remarks on another page, the more miserly a man is, the more good he does. The second motive "is the most dangerous one to which society is exposed." Love is all very pretty: "no higher or purer source of human happiness exists." (Ahem!) But it is a "source of enduring injury," and, in short, should be overruled by something wiser. What is this wiser motive? We shall see.

As for public-spirit, it is rendered nugatory by the "difficulties in the way of its effective operation." For example, it might suggest putting checks upon the fecundity of the poor and the vicious; and "no measure of repression would be too severe," in the case of criminals. The hint is broad. But unfortunately, you cannot induce legislatures to take such measures, owing to the pestiferous "tender sentiments of man towards man." It thus appears that public-spirit, or Benthamism, is not strong enough to be the effective tutor of love (I am skipping to another page), which must therefore be handed over to "the motives which animate men in the pursuit of wealth," in which alone we can confide, and which "are in the highest degree beneficent."[1] Yes, in the "highest degree" without exception are they beneficent to the being upon whom all their blessings are poured out, namely, the Self, whose "sole object," says the writer, in accumulating wealth is his individual "sustenance and enjoyment." Plainly, the author holds the no-

tion that some other motive might be in a higher degree beneficent even for the man's self to be a paradox wanting in good sense. He seeks to gloze and modify his doctrine; but he lets the perspicacious reader see what his animating principle is; and when, holding the opinions I have repeated, he at the same time acknowledges that society could not exist upon a basis of intelligent greed alone, he simply pigeon-holes himself as one of the eclectics of inharmonious opinions. He wants his mammon flavored with a *soupçon* of god.

The economists accuse those to whom the enunciation of their atrocious villainies communicates a thrill of horror of being *sentimentalists*. It may be so: I willingly confess to having some tincture of sentimentalism in me, God be thanked! Ever since the French Revolution brought this leaning of thought into ill-repute, — and not altogether undeservedly, I must admit, true, beautiful, and good as that great movement was, — it has been the tradition to picture sentimentalists as persons incapable of logical thought and unwilling to look facts in the eyes. This tradition may be classed with the French tradition that an Englishman says *godam* at every second sentence, the English tradition that an American talks about "Britishers," and the American tradition that a Frenchman carries forms of etiquette to an inconvenient extreme, in short with all those traditions which survive simply because the men who use their eyes and ears are few and far between. Doubtless some excuse there was for all those opinions in days gone by; and sentimentalism, when it was the fashionable amusement to spend one's evenings in a flood of tears over a woeful performance on a candle-litten stage, sometimes made itself a little ridiculous. But what after all is sentimentalism? It is

[1] How can a writer have any respect for science, as such, who is capable of confounding with the scientific propositions of political economy, which have nothing to say concerning what is "beneficent," such brummagem generalisations as this?

an *ism,* a doctrine, namely, the doctrine that great respect should be paid to the natural judgments of the sensible heart. This is what sentimentalism precisely is; and I entreat the reader to consider whether to contemn it is not of all blasphemies the most degrading. Yet the nineteenth century has steadily contemned it, because it brought about the Reign of Terror. That it did so is true. Still, the whole question is one of *how much.* The reign of terror was very bad; but now the Gradgrind banner has been this century long flaunting in the face of heaven, with an insolence to provoke the very skies to scowl and rumble. Soon a flash and quick peal will shake economists quite out of their complacency, too late. The twentieth century, in its latter half, shall surely see the deluge-tempest burst upon the social order, — to clear upon a world as deep in ruin as that greed-philosophy has long plunged it into guilt. No post-thermidorian high jinks then!

So a miser is a beneficent power in a community, is he? With the same reason precisely, only in a much higher degree, you might pronounce the Wall Street sharp to be a good angel, who takes money from heedless persons not likely to guard it properly, who wrecks feeble enterprises better stopped, and who administers wholesome lessons to unwary scientific men, by passing worthless checks upon them, — as you did, the other day, to me, my millionaire Master in glomery, when you thought you saw your way to using my process without paying for it, and of so bequeathing to your children something to boast of their father about, — and who by a thousand wiles puts money at the service of intelligent greed, in his own person. Bernard Mandeville, in his "Fable of the Bees," maintains that private vices of all descriptions are public benefits, and proves it, too, quite as cogently as the economist proves his point concerning the miser. He even argues, with no slight force, that but for vice civilisation would never have existed. In the same spirit, it has been strongly maintained and is to-day widely believed that all acts of charity and benevolence, private and public, go seriously to degrade the human race.

The "Origin of Species" of Darwin merely extends politico-economical views of progress to the entire realm of animal and vegetable life. The vast majority of our contemporary naturalists hold the opinion that the true cause of those exquisite and marvellous adaptations of nature for which, when I was a boy, men used to extol the divine wisdom is that creatures are so crowded together that those of them that happen to have the slightest advantage force those less pushing into situations unfavorable to multiplication or even kill them before they reach the age of reproduction. Among animals, the mere mechanical individualism is vastly reënforced as a power making for good by the animal's ruthless greed. As Darwin puts it on his title-page, it is the struggle for existence; and he should have added for his motto: Every individual for himself, and the Devil take the hindmost! Jesus, in his sermon on the Mount, expressed a different opinion.

Here, then, is the issue. The gospel of Christ says that progress comes from every individual merging his individuality in sympathy with his neighbors. On the other side, the conviction of the nineteenth century is that progress takes place by virtue of every individual's striving for himself with all his might and trampling his neighbor under foot whenever he gets a chance to do so. This may accurately be called the Gospel of Greed.

W. J. Ghent: THE NEXT STEP:
A BENEVOLENT FEUDALISM

THE next distinct stage in the socio-economic evolution of America may be something entirely different from any of the forms usually predicted. Anarchist prophecies are, of course, futile; and the Tolstoyan Utopia of a return to primitive production, with its prodigal waste of effort and consequent impoverishment of the race, allures but few minds. The Kropotkinian dream of a communistic union of shop industry and agriculture is of a like type; and well-nigh as barren are the Neo-Jeffersonian visions of a general revival of small-farm and small-shop production and the dominance of a middle-class democracy. The orthodox economists, with their notions of a slightly modified Individualism, wherein each unit secures the just reward of his capacity and service, are but worshipping an image which they have created out of their books, and which has no real counterpart in life; and finally, the Marxists, who predict the establishment of a co-operative commonwealth are, to say the least, too sanguine in foreshortening the time of its triumph. Whatever the more distant future may bring to pass, there is but little evidence to prove that collectivism will be the next status of society. Rather, that coming status, of which the contributing forces are now energetically at work and of which the first phases are already plainly observa-ble, will be something in the nature of a Benevolent Feudalism.

That the concentration of capital and the increase of individual holdings of wealth will continue is almost unanimously conceded. Forty years ago Marx laid down the formula of capitalist accumulation which has ever since been a fixed article of creed with the orthodox Socialists. "One capitalist always kills many" is its central maxim. And only recently Prof. John B. Clark, doubtless our most distinguished representative of the orthodox economists, declared, in the pages of *The Independent*, that

the world of the near future . . . will present a condition of vast and ever-growing inequality. . . . The rich will continually grow richer, and the multi-millionaires will approach the billion-dollar standard.

It is a view that needs no particular buttressing of authority, for it is held by most of those who seriously scan the outlook.

There are, it is not to be disputed, certain tendencies and data which apparently conflict with this view. There is a marked persistence, and in some cases a growth, of small-unit farming and of small-shop production and distribution. This tendency is strongly insisted upon by Prince Kropotkin and by the German

From *The Independent*, 54 (April 3, 1902), 781–788.

Socialist Bernstein, and is conceded, tho cautiously, by a number of other radicals, among them the Belgian Socialist Vandervelde. That it is a real tendency seems unquestioned on the face of the figures from Germany, France, England and Belgium; and it is not unlikely that further confirmation will be found in the detailed reports of the last United States census. Furthermore, the great commercial combinations are not necessarily a proof of individual increase of wealth. Often, perhaps generally, they result in this individual increase; but the two things are not inevitably related. These combinations are generally, as William Graham pointed out nearly twelve years ago, a massing together of separate portions of capital, small, great and moderate — a union of capitals for a common purpose while still separately owned. Lipton's great company, for instance, has over 62,000 shareholders; and many of America's most powerful combinations are built up out of a multitude of small and moderate holdings.

But tho these facts and tendencies be admitted, they do not really affect the foregoing generalization. The drift toward small-unit production and distribution in certain lines argues no growth of economic independence. On the contrary, it is attended by a constant pressure and constraint. The more the great combinations increase their power, the greater is the subordination of the small concerns. They may, for one reason or another, find it possible, and even fairly profitable, to continue; but they will be more and more confined to particular activities, to particular territories, and in time to particular methods, all dictated and enforced by the pressure of the larger concerns. The petty tradesmen and producers are thus an economically de-

pendent class; and their dependence increases with the years. In a like position, also, are the owners of small and moderate holdings in the trusts. The larger holdings — often the single largest holding — determines the rules of the game; the smaller ones are either acquiescent, or if recalcitrant, are powerless to enforce their will. Especially is this true in America, where the head of a corporation is often an absolute ruler, who determines not only the policy of the enterprise, but the *personnel* of the board of directors.

The tendencies thus make, on the one hand, toward the centralization of vast power in the hands of a few men — the morganization of industry, as it were — and on the other, toward a vast increase in the number of those who compose the economically dependent classes. The latter number is already stupendous. The laborers and mechanics were long ago brought under the yoke through their divorcement from the land and the application of steam to factory operation. They are economically unfree except in so far as their organizations make possible a collective bargaining for wages and hours. The growth of commerce raised up an enormous class of clerks and helpers, perhaps the most dependent class in the community. The growth and partial diffusion of wealth in America has in fifty years largely altered the character of domestic service and increased the number of servants many fold. Railroad pools and farm-implement trusts have drawn a tightening cordon about the farmers. The professions, too, have felt the change. Behind many of our important newspapers are private commercial interests which dictate their general policy, if not, as is frequently the case, their particular attitude upon every public question;

while the race for endowments made by the greater number of the churches and by all colleges except a few State-supported ones, compels a cautious regard on the part of synod and faculty for the wishes, the views and prejudices of men of great wealth. To this growing deference of preacher, teacher and editor is added that of two yet more important classes — the makers and the interpreters of law. The record of legislation and judicial interpretation regarding slavery previous to the Civil War has been paralleled in recent years by the record of legislatures and courts in matters relating to the lives and health of manual workers, especially in such cases as employers' liability and factory inspection. Thus, with a great addition to the number of subordinate classes, with a tremendous increase of their individual components, and with a corresponding growth of power in the hands of a few score magnates, there is needed little further to make up a socio-economic status that contains all the essentials of a renascent feudalism.

It is, at least in its beginning, less a personal than a class feudalism. History may repeat itself, as the adage runs; but not by identical forms and events. The great spirals of evolutionary progress carry us for a time back to the general direction of older journeyings, but not to the well-worn pathways themselves. The old feudalism exacted faithful service, industrial and martial, from the underling; protection and justice from the overlord. It is not likely that personal fidelity, as once known, can ever be restored: the long period of dislodgment from the land, the diffusion of learning, the exercise of the franchise, and the training in individual effort have left a seemingly unbridgeable chasm between the past and the present forms.

But tho personal fidelity, in the old sense, is improbable, group fidelity, founded upon the conscious dependence of a class, is already observable, and it grows apace. Out of the sense of class dependence arises the extreme deference which we yield, the rapt homage which we pay — not as individuals, but as units of a class — to the men of wealth. We do not know them personally, and we have no sense of personal attachment. But in most things we grant them priority. We send them or their legates to the Senate to make our laws; we permit them to name our administrators and our judiciary; we listen with eager attention to their utterances and we abide by their judgment. Not always, indeed; for some of us grumble at times and ask angrily where it will all end. We talk threateningly of instituting referendums to curb excessive power; of levying income taxes, or of compelling the Government to acquire the railroads and the telegraphs. We subscribe to newspapers and other publications which criticise the acts of the great corporations, and we hail as a new Gracchus the ardent reformer who occasionally comes forth for a season to do battle for the popular cause. But this revolt is, for the most part, sentimental; it is a mental attitude but rarely transmutable into terms of action. It is, moreover, sporadic and flickering; it dies out after a time, and we revert to our usual moods, concerning ourselves with our particular interests and letting the rest of the world wag as it will.

The new feudalism is thus characterized by a class dependence rather than by a personal dependence. But it differs in still other respects from the old. It is qualified and restricted, and by agencies hardly operative in medieval times. Democracy tends to restrain it, and ethics to moralize it. Tho it has its birth and nurture out of the "rough and unsocialized barbarians of wealth," in Mr. Henry D. Lloyd's phrase, its youth and maturity promise a modification of character. More and more it tends to become a *benevolent* feudalism. On the ethical side it is qualified by a growing and diffusive sense of responsibility and of kinship. The principle of the "trusteeship of great wealth," having found lodgment, like a seed, in the erstwhile barren soil of mammonism, has become a flourishing growth. The enormous benefactions for social purposes, which have been common of late years, and which in 1901 reached a total of $107,000,000, could come only from men and women who have been taught to feel an ethical duty to society. It is a duty, true enough, which is but dimly seen and imperfectly fulfilled. The greater part of these benefactions is directed to purposes which have but a slight or indirect bearing upon the relief of social distress, the restraint of injustice, or the mitigation of remediable hardships. The giving is even often economically false, and if carried to an extreme would prove disastrous to the community; for in many cases it is a transmutation of wealth from a status of active capital, wherein it makes possible a greater diffusion of comfort, to a status of comparative sterility. But, tho often mistaken as is the conception and futile the fulfilment of this duty, the fact that it is apprehended at all is one of far-reaching importance.

The limitation which democracy puts upon the new feudalism is also important. For democracy will endure, in spite of the new order. "Like death," said Disraeli, "it gives back nothing." Something of its substance it gives back, it must be confessed; for it permits the most serious encroachments upon its rights; but of its outer forms it yields nothing, and thus it retains the potentiality of exerting its will in whatever direction it may see fit. And this fact, tho now but feebly recognized by the feudal barons, will be better understood by them as time runs on, and they will bear in mind the limit of popular patience. It is an elastic limit, of a truth; for the mass of mankind, as both Hamlet and Thomas Jefferson observed, are more ready to endure known ills than to fly to others that they know not. It is a limit which, to be heeded, needs only to be carefully studied. Macaulay's famous dictum, that the privileged classes, when their rule is threatened, always bring about their own ruin by making further exactions, is likely, in this case, to prove untrue. A wiser forethought begins to prevail among the autocrats of to-day — a forethought destined to grow and expand and to prove of inestimable value when bequeathed to their successors. Our nobility will thus temper their exactions to an endurable limit; and they will distribute benefits to a degree that makes a tolerant, if not a satisfied people. They may even make a working principle of Bentham's maxim, and after, of course, appropriating the first and choicest fruits of industry to themselves, may seek to promote the "greatest happiness of the greatest number." For therein will lie their greater security.

Of the particular forms which this new feudalism will take there are already numerous indications which furnish grounds for more or less confident prediction. All societies evolve naturally out of their predecessors. In sociology, as in biology, there is no cell without a parent cell. The society of each generation develops a multitude of spontaneous and acquired variations, and out of these, by a blending process of natural and conscious selection, the succeeding society is evolved. The new feudalism is but an orderly outgrowth of past and present tendencies and conditions.

Unlike the old feudalism it is not confined to the country. Qualified in certain respects tho it be, it has yet a far wider province and scope of action. The great manorial estates now being created along the banks of the Hudson, along the shores of Long Island Sound and Lake Michigan, are but its pleasure places — its Sans Soucis, its Bagatelles. For from being the foundation of its revenues, as were the estates of the old feudalism, these are the prodigally expensive playthings of the new. The oil wells, the mines, the grain fields, the forests and the great thoroughfares of the land are its ultimate sources of revenue; but its strongholds are in the cities. It is in these centers of activity, with their warehouses, where the harvests are hoarded; their workshops, where the metals and woods are fashioned into articles of use; their great distributing houses; their exchanges; their enormously valuable franchises to be had for the asking or the seizing, and their pressure of population, which forces an hourly increase in the exorbitant value of land, that the new feudalism finds the field best adapted for its main operations.

Bondage to the land was the basis of villeinage in the old *régime;* bondage to the job will be the basis of villeinage in the new. The wage-system will endure, for it is an incomparably simpler means of determining the baron's volume of profits than were the "boon-works," the "week-works" and the *corvées* of old. But with increasing concentration on the one hand, and the fiercer competition for employment on the other, the secured job will become the laborer's fortress, which he will hardly dare to evacuate.

The hope of bettering his condition by surrendering one place in the expectation of getting another will be qualified by a restraining prudence. He will no longer trust his individual strength, but will protest against ill conditions, or, in the last resort, strike, only in company with a formidable host of his fellows. And even the collective assertion of his demands will be restrained more and more as he considers recurring failures of his efforts such as that of the recent steel strike. Moreover, concentration gives opportunity for an almost indefinite extension of the blacklist: a person of offensive activity may be denied work in every feudal shop and on every feudal farm from one end of the country to the other. He will be a hardy and reckless industrial villein indeed who will dare incur the enmity of the Duke of the Oil Trust when he knows that his actions will be promptly communicated to the banded autocracy of dukes, earls and marquises of the steel, coal, iron, window glass, lumber and traffic industries.

Of the three under classes of the old feudalism — sub-tenants, cotters and villeins — the first two are already on the ground, and the last is in process of restoration. But the vast complexity of modern society specializes functions, and for the new feudalism still other classes are required. It is a difficult task properly to differentiate these classes. They shade off almost imperceptibly into one another; and the dynamic processes of modern industry often hurl, in one mighty convulsion, great bodies of individuals from a higher to a lower class, blurring or obscuring the lines of demarcation. Nevertheless, to take a figure from geology, these convulsions become less and less frequent as the substratum of industrial processes becomes more fixed and regular; the classes become more stable and show more distinct differences, and they will tend, under the new *régime,* to the formal institution of graded caste. At the bottom are the wastrels, at the top the barons; and the gradation, when the new *régime* shall have become fully developed, whole and perfect in its parts, will be about as follows:

I. The barons, graded on the basis of possessions.

II. The courtiers and court-agents.

III. The workers in pure and applied science, artists and physicians. The new feudalism, like most autocracies, will foster not only the arts, but also certain kinds of learning — particularly the kinds which are unlikely to disturb the minds of the multitude. A future Marsh or Cope or Le Conte will be liberally patronized and left free to discover what he will; and so, too, an Edison or a Marconi. Only they must not meddle with anything relating to social science. For obvious reasons, also, physicians will occupy a position of honor and comparative freedom under the new *régime.*

IV. The *entrepreneurs,* the managers of the great industries, transformed into a salaried class.

V. The foremen and superintendents. This class has heretofore been recruited largely from the skilled workers, but with the growth of technical education in schools and colleges and the development of fixed caste, it is likely to become entirely differentiated.

VI. The villeins of the cities and towns, more or less regularly employed, who do skilled work and are partially protected by organization.

VII. The villeins of the cities and towns who do unskilled work and are unprotected by organization. They will comprise the laborers, domestics and clerks.

VIII. The villeins of the manorial estates, of the great farms, the mines and the forests.

IX. The small-unit farmers (landowning), the petty tradesmen and manufacturers.

X. The sub-tenants on the manorial estates and great farms (corresponding to the class of "free tenants" in the old feudalism).

XI. The cotters, living in isolated places and on the margin of cultivation.

XII. The tramps, the occasionally employed, the unemployed — the wastrels of city and country.

This, then, is the table of socio-industrial rank leading down from the feudatory barons. It is a classification open, of course, to amendment. The minor shareholders, it may be suggested, are not provided for; and certain other omissions might be named. But it is not possible to anticipate every detail; and, as for the small shareholders, who now occupy a wide range, from comparative poverty to comparative affluence, it seems likely that the complete development of the new *régime* will practically eliminate them. Other critics, furthermore, will object to the basis of gradation. The basis employed is not relative wealth, a test which nine out of ten persons would unhesitatingly apply in social classification; it is not comparative earning capacity, economic freedom, nor intellectual ability. Rather, it is the relative degree of comfort — material, moral and intellectual — which each class contributes to the nobility. The wastrels contribute least, and they are the lowest. The foremen, superintendents and *entrepreneurs* contribute most of the purely material comfort, and their place is correspondingly high. But higher yet is the rank of the courtiers and court agents, the legates and nuncios. This class will include the editors of "respectable" and "safe" news-papers, the pastors of "conservative" and "wealthy" churches, the professors and teachers in endowed colleges and schools, lawyers generally, and most judges and politicians. During the transition period there will be a gradual elimination of the more unserviceable of these persons, with the result that in the end this class will be largely transformed. The individual security of place and livelihood of its members will then depend on the harmony of their utterances and acts with the wishes of the great nobles; and so long as they rightly fulfil their functions their recompense will be generous. They will be at once the assuagers of popular suspicion and discontent and the providers of moral and intellectual anodynes for the barons. Such of them, however, as have not the tact or fidelity to do or say what is expected of them will be promptly forced into class XI or XII, or, in extreme cases, banished from all classes, to become the wretched pariahs of society.

Through all the various activities of these populous classes (except the last) our Benevolent Feudalism will carry on the nation's work. Its operations will begin with the land, whence it extracts the raw material of commerce. It is just at this stage of its workings that it will differ most from the customary forms of the old. The cotters will be pushed further back into isolation, and the sub-tenants will be confined to the grubbing away at their ill-recompensed labors. It is with the eighth class, the villeins of farm and wood and mine, that we have here to deal. The ancient ceremony of "homage," the swearing of personal fidelity to the lord, is transformed into that of the beseeching of the foreman for work. The wage system, with its mechanical simplicity, continuing in force,

there is an absence of the old exactions of special work from the employed villein. A mere altering of the wage scale appropriates to the great noble whatever share of the product he feels he may safely demand for himself. Thus "week-work," the three or four days' toil in each week which the villein had to give unrecompensed to the lord, and "boon-work," the several days of extra toil three or four times a year, will never be revived. Even the company store, the modern form of feudal exaction, will in time be given up, for at best it is but a clumsy and offensive makeshift, and defter and less irritating means are at hand for reaching the same result. There will hardly be a restoration of "relief," the payment of a year's dues on inheriting an allotment of land, or of "heriot," the payment of a valuable gift from the possessions of a deceased relative. Indeed, these tithes may not be worth the bother of collecting; for the villein's inheritance will probably be but moderate, as befits his state and the place which God and the nobility have ordained for him.

The raw materials gathered, the scene of operations shifts from the country to the cities and great towns. But many of the latter will lose, during the transition period, a considerable part of their greatness, from the shutting up of needless factories and the concentration of production in the larger workshops. There will thus be large displacements of labor, and for a time a wide extension of suffering. Popular discontent will naturally follow, and it will be fomented, to some extent, by agitation; but the agitation will be guarded in expression and action, and it will be relatively barren of result. The possible danger therefrom will have been provided against, and a host of economists, preachers and editors will be ready to show indisputably that the evolution taking place is for the best interests of all; that it follows a "natural and inevitable law"; that those who have been thrown out of work have only their own incompetency to blame; that all who really want work can get it, and that any interference with the prevailing *régime* will be sure to bring on a panic, which will only make matters worse. Hearing this, the multitude will hesitatingly acquiesce and thereupon subside; and tho occasionally a radical journal or a radical agitator will counsel revolt, the mass will remain quiescent. Gradually, too, by one method or another, sometimes by the direct action of the nobility, the greater part of the displaced workers will find some means of getting bread, while those who cannot will be eliminated from the struggle and cease to be a potential factor for trouble.

In its general aspects shop industry will be carried on much as now. Only the shops will be very much larger, the individual and total output will be greater, the unit cost of production will be lessened. Wages and hours will for a time continue on something like the present level; but, despite the persistence of the unions, no considerable gains in behalf of labor are to be expected. The owners of all industry worth owning, the barons will laugh at threats of striking and boycotting. No competitor can possibly make capital out of the labor disputes of another, for there will be no competitors, actual or potential. What the barons will most dread will be the collective assertion of the villeins at the polls; but this, from experience, they will know to be a thing of no immediate danger. By the putting forward of a hundred irrelevant issues they can hopelessly divide the voters at each election; or, that failing, there is always to be

trusted as a last resort the cry of impending panic.

Practically all industry will be regulated in terms of wages, and the *entrepreneurs,* who will then have become the chief salaried officers of the nobles, will calculate to a hair the needful production for each year. Waste and other losses will thus be reduced to a minimum. A vast scheme of exact systematization will have taken the place of the old free competition, and industry will be carried on as by clockwork.

Gradually a change will take place in the aspirations and conduct of the younger generations. Heretofore there has been at least some degree of freedom of choice in determining one's occupation, however much that freedom has been curtailed by actual economic conditions. But with the settling of industrial processes comes more and more constraint. The dream of the children of the farms to escape from their drudgery by migrating to the city, and from the stepping stone of a clerkly place at $3 a week to rise to affluence, will be given over, and they will follow the footsteps of their fathers. A like fixity of condition will be observed in the cities, and the sons of clerks and of mechanics and of day laborers will tend to accept their environment of birth and training and abide by it. It is a phenomenon observable in all countries where the economic pressure is severe, and it is certain to obtain in feudal America.

The sub-tenants and the small-unit producers and distributers will be confined within smaller and smaller limits, while the foremen, the superintendents and the *entrepreneurs* of the workshops will attain to greater power and recompense. But the chief glory of the new *régime,* next to that of the nobles, will be that of the class of courtiers and court-agents. Theirs, in a sense, will be the most important function in the State — "to justify the ways of God [and the nobility] to man." Two divisions of the courtier class, however, will find life rather a burdensome travail. They are the judges and the politicians. Holding their places at once by popular election and by the grace of the barons, they will be fated to a constant see-saw of conflicting obligations. They must, in some measure, satisfy the demands of the multitude, and yet, on the other hand, they must obey the commands from above.

The outlines of the present State loom but feebly through the intricate network of the new system. The nobles will have attained to complete power, and the motive and operation of Government will have become simply the registering and administering of their collective will. And yet the State will continue very much as now, just as the form and name of the Roman Republic continued under Augustus. The present State machinery is admirably adapted for the subtle and extra-legal exertion of power by an autocracy; and while improvements to that end might unquestionably be made, the barons will hesitate to take action which will needlessly arouse popular suspicions. From petty constable to Supreme Court Justice the officials will understand, or be made to understand, the golden mean of their duties; and except for an occasional rascally Jacobin, whom it may for a time be difficult to suppress, they will be faithful and obey.

The manorial courts, with powers exercised by the local lords, will not, as a rule, be restored. Probably the "court baron," for determining tenantry and wage questions, will be revived. It may even come as a natural outgrowth of the present conciliation boards, with a successor of the Committee of Thirty-six as a sort of general court baron for the nation. But the "court leet," the manorial institution for punishing misdemeanors, wherein the baron holds his powers by special grant from the central authority of the State, we shall never know again. It is far simpler and will be less disturbing to the popular mind to leave in existence the present courts so long as the baron can dictate the general policy of justice.

Armed force will, of course, be employed to overawe the discontented and to quiet unnecessary turbulence. Unlike the armed forces of the old feudalism, the nominal control will be that of the State; the soldiery will be regular and not irregular. Not again will the barons risk the general indignation arising from the employment of Pinkertons and other private armies. The worker has unmistakably shown his preference, when he is to be subdued, for the militia and the Federal army. Broadly speaking, it is not an unreasonable attitude; and it goes without saying that it will be respected. The militia of our Benevolent Feudalism will be recruited, as now, mostly from the clerkly class; and it will be officered largely by the sons and nephews of the barons. But its actions will be tempered by a saner policy. Governed by those who have most to fear from popular exasperation, it will show a finer restraint.

A general view of the new society will present little of startling novelty. A person leaving this planet to-day and revisiting "the pale glimpses of the moon" when the new order is in full swing will from superficial observation see but few changes. *Alter et idem* — another, yet the same — he will say. Only by closer view will he mark the deepening and widening of channels along which the powerful currents of present tendencies are borne; only so will he note the effect of the more complete development of the mighty forces now at work.

So comprehensive and so exact will be the social and political control that it will be exercised in a constantly widening scope and over a growing multiplicity of details. The distribution of wages and dividends will be nicely balanced with a watchful regard for possible dissatisfaction. Old-age pensions to the more faithful employees, such as those granted by the Illinois Central, the Pennsylvania, the Colorado Fuel & Iron Company, the Metropolitan Traction Company, or the Lackawanna, will be generally distributed, for the hard work will be done only by the most vigorous, and a large class of destitute unemployed will be a needless menace to the *régime*. Peace will be the main desideratum, and its cultivation will be the most honored science of the age. A happy blending of generosity and firmness will characterize all dealings with open discontent; but the prevention of discontent will be the prior study, to which the intellect and the energies of the nobles and their legates will be ever bent. To that end the teachings of the schools and colleges, the sermons, the editorials, the stump orations, and even the plays at the theaters will be skilfully and persuasively molded; and the questioning heart of the poor, which perpetually seeks some answer to the painful riddle of the earth, will meet with a multitude of mollifying responses. These will be: From the churches, that discontent is the fruit of atheism, and that religion alone is a solace for earthly wo; from the colleges, that discontent is ignorant and irrational, since conditions have certainly bettered in the last one hundred years; from the newspapers, that discontent is anarchy; and from the stump orators that it is unpatriotic, since this nation is the greatest and most glorious that ever

the sun shone upon. As of old, these reasons will for the time suffice; and against the possibility of recurrent questionings new apologetics will be skilfully formulated, to be put forth as occasion requires. On all sides will be observed a greater respect for power; and the former tendency toward rash and bitter criticism of the upper classes will decline.

The arts, too, will be modified. Literature will take on the hues and tones of the good-natured days of Charles II. Instead of poetry, however, the innocuous novel will flourish best; every flowery courtier will write romance, and the literary darling of the renascence will be an Edmund Waller of fiction. A lineal descendant of the famous Lely, who

> . . . on animated canvas stole
> The sleepy eye that spoke the melting soul,

will be the laureled chief of our painters; and sculpture, architecture and the lesser arts, under the spell of changed influences, will undergo a like transformation.

This, then, in the rough, is our Benevolent Feudalism to-be. It is not precisely a Utopia, not an "island valley of Avilion"; and yet it has its commendable, even its fascinating features. "The empire is peace," shouted the partisans of Louis Napoleon; and a like cry, with an equal ardency of enthusiasm, will be uttered by the supporters of the new *régime*. Peace and stability will be its defensive arguments, and peace and stability it will probably bring. But tranquil or unquiet, whatever it may be, its triumph is assured; and existent forces are carrying us toward it with an ever accelerating speed. One power alone might prevent it — the collective popular will that it shall not be. But of this there is no fear on the part of the barons, and but little expectation on the part of the underlings.

Thorstein Veblen: THE CAPTAIN OF INDUSTRY

THE Captain of Industry is one of the major institutions of the nineteenth century. He has been an institution of civilised life — a self-sufficient element in the scheme of law and custom — in much the same sense as the Crown, or the Country Gentleman, or the Priesthood, have been institutions, or as they still are in those places where the habits of thought which they embody still have an institutional force.[1] For a hundred years or so he was, cumulatively, the dominant figure in civilised life, about whose deeds and interests law and custom have turned, the central and paramount personal agency in Occidental civilisation. Indeed, his great vogue and compelling eminence are not past yet, so far as regards his place in popular superstition and in the make-believe of political strategy, but it is essentially a glory standing over out of the past, essentially a superstition.[2] As regards the material actualities of life, the captain of industry is no longer the central and directive force in that business traffic that governs the material fortunes of mankind; not much more so than the Crown, the Country Gentleman, or the Priesthood.

[1] An institution is of the nature of a usage which has become axiomatic and indispensable by habituation and general acceptance. Its physiological counterpart would presumably be any one of those habitual addictions that are now attracting the attention of the experts in sobriety.

[2] He is also still a dominant figure in the folklore of Political Economy.

Considered as an institution, then, the captain of industry is the personal upshot of that mobilisation of business enterprise that arose out of the industrial use of the machine process. And the period of his ascendency is, accordingly, that era of (temperately) free competition that lies between the Industrial Revolution of the eighteenth century and the rise of corporation finance in the nineteenth, and so tapering off into the competitive twilight-zone of the later time when competition was shifting from industry to finance. But in the time of his ascendency the old-fashioned competitive system came up, flourished, and eventually fell into decay, all under the ministering hand of the Captain.

As is likely to be true of any institution that eventually counts for much in human life and culture, so also the captain of industry arose out of small beginnings which held no clear promise of a larger destiny. The prototype rather than the origin of the captain of industry is to be seen in the Merchant Adventurer of an earlier age, or as he would be called after he had grown to larger dimensions and become altogether sessile, the Merchant Prince. In the beginning the captain was an adventurer in industrial enterprise — hence the name given him; very much as the itinerant merchant of the days of the petty trade had once been an adventurer in commerce. He was a person of insight

— perhaps chiefly industrial insight — and of initiative and energy, who was able to see something of the industrial reach and drive of that new mechanical technology that was finding its way into the industries, and who went about to contrive ways and means of turning these technological resources to new uses and a larger efficiency; always with a view to his own gain from turning out a more serviceable product with greater expedition. He was a captain of workmanship at the same time that he was a business man; but he was a good deal of a pioneer in both respects, inasmuch as he was on new ground in both respects. In many of the industrial ventures into which his initiative led him, both the mechanical working and the financial sanity of the new ways and means were yet to be tried out, so that in both respects he was working out an adventurous experiment rather than watchfully waiting for the turn of events. In the typical case, he was business manager of the venture as well as foreman of the works, and not infrequently he was the designer and masterbuilder of the equipment, of which he was also the responsible owner.[3] Typical of the work and spirit of these Captains of the early time are the careers of the great tool-builders of the late eighteenth and early nineteenth century.[4]

Such, it is believed, were many of those to whom the mechanical industries owed their rapid growth and sweeping success in the early time, both in production and in earning-capacity; and something of this sort is the typical Captain of Industry as he has lived, and still lives, in the affections of his countrymen. Such also is the type-form in terms of which those

[3] Cf. *The Engineers and the Price System*, ch. ii. "The Industrial System and the Captains of Industry."

[4] Cf. Roe, *British and American Tool-Builders.*

substantial citizens like to think of themselves, who aspire to the title. If this characterisation may appear large and fanciful to an unbelieving generation, at least the continued vogue of it both as a popular superstition and as a business man's day-dream will go to show that the instinct of workmanship is not dead yet even in those civilised countries where it has become eternally right and good that workmanship should wait on business. The disposition to think kindly of workmanlike service is still extant in these civilised nations, at least in their day-dreams; although business principles have put it in abeyance so far as regards any practical effect.

In fact, it seems to be true that many, perhaps most, of those persons who amassed fortunes out of the proceeds of industry during this early period (say, 1760–1860), and who thereby acquired merit, were not of this workmanlike or pioneering type, but rather came in for large gains by shrewd investment and conservative undertakings, such as would now be called safe and sane business. Yet there will at the same time also have been so much of this spirit of initiative and adventure abroad in the conduct of industry, and it will have been so visible an element of industrial business-as-usual at that time, as to have enabled this type-form of the captain of industry to find lodgment in the popular belief; a man of workmanlike force and creative insight into the community's needs, who stood out on a footing of self-help, took large chances for large ideals, and came in for his gains as a due reward for work well done in the service of the common good, in designing and working out a more effective organisation of industrial forces and in creating and testing out new and better processes of production. It is by no means easy at this distance to make out how much of popular myth-making went to set up this genial conception of the Captain in the popular mind, or how much more of the same engaging conceit was contributed toward the same preconception by the many-sided self-esteem of many substantial business men who had grown great by "buying in" and "sitting tight," and who would like to believe that they had done something to merit their gains. But however the balance may lie, between workmanship and salesmanship, in the make-up of the common run of those early leaders of industrial enterprise, it seems that there will have been enough of the master-workman in a sufficient number of them, and enough of adventure and initiative in a sufficient number of the undertakings, to enable the popular fancy to set up and hold fast this genial belief in the typical captain of industry as a creative factor in the advance of the industrial arts; at the same time that the economists were able presently to set him up, under the name of "Entrepreneur," as a fourth factor of production, along with Land, Labor, and Capital. Indeed, it is on some such ground that men have come to be called "Captains of Industry" rather than captains of business. Experience and observation at any later period could scarcely have engendered such a conception of those absentee owners who control the country's industrial plant and trade on a restricted output.

By insensible degrees, as the volume of industry grew larger, employing a larger equipment and larger numbers of workmen, the business concerns necessarily also increased in size and in the volume of transactions, personal supervision of the work by the owners was no longer practicable, and personal contact and personal arrangements between the employer-owner and his workmen tapered off into impersonal wage contracts governed by custom and adjusted to the minimum which the traffic would bear. The employer-owner, an ever increasingly impersonal business concern, shifted more and more to a footing of accountancy in its relations with the industrial plant and its personnel, and the oversight of the works passed by insensible degrees into the hands of technical experts who stood in a business relation to the concern, as its employees responsible to the concern for working the plant to such a fraction of its productive capacity as the condition of the market warranted for the time being.

So the function of the entrepreneur, the captain of industry, gradually fell apart in a two-fold division of labor, between the business manager and the office work on the one side and the technician and industrial work on the other side. Gradually more and more, by this shift and division, the captain of industry developed into a captain of business, and that part of his occupation which had given him title to his name and rank as captain of "industry" passed into alien hands. Expert practical men, practical in the way of tangible performance, men who had, or need have, no share in the prospective net gain and no responsibility for the concern's financial transactions, unbusinesslike technicians, began to be drawn into the management of the industry on the tangible side. It was a division of labor and responsibility, between the employer-owners who still were presumed to carry on the business of the concern and who were responsible to themselves for its financial fortunes, and on the other hand the expert industrial men who took over the tangible performance of production and were responsible to their own sense of workmanship.

Industry and business gradually split apart, in so far as concerned the personnel and the day's work. The employer-owners, shifted farther over on their own ground as absentee owners, but continued to govern the volume of production and the conditions of life for the working personnel on the businesslike principle of the net gain in terms of price. While the tangible performance of so much work as the absentee owners considered to be wise, fell increasingly under the management of that line of technicians out of which there grew in time the engineering profession, with its many duties, grades, and divisions and its ever increasingly numerous and increasingly specialised personnel. It was a gradual shift and division, of course. So gradual, indeed, that while it had set in in a small way before the close of the eighteenth century, it had not yet been carried out completely and obviously by the close of the nineteenth, even in the greater mechanical industries. In fact, it has not yet been carried through to so rigorous a finish as to have warranted its recognition in the standard economic theories. In the manuals the captain of industry still figures as the enterprising investor-technician of the days of the beginning, and as such he still is a certified article of economic doctrine under the caption of the "Entrepreneur."

The industrial arts are a matter of tangible performance directed to work that is designed to be of material use to man, and all the while they are calling for an increasingly exhaustive knowledge of material fact and an increasingly close application to the work in hand. The realities of the technician's world are mechanistic realities, matters of material fact. And the responsibilities of the technician, as such, are responsibilities of workmanship only; in the last resort responsibility to his own sense of workmanlike performance, which might well be called the engineer's conscience. On the

other hand the arts of business are arts of bargaining, effrontery, salesmanship, make-believe, and are directed to the gain of the business man at the cost of the community, at large and in detail. Neither tangible performance nor the common good is a business proposition. Any material use which his traffic may serve is quite beside the business man's purpose, except indirectly, in so far as it may serve to influence his clientele to his advantage.

But the arts of business, too, call all the while for closer application to the work in hand. Throughout recent times salesmanship has come in for a steadily increasing volume and intensity of attention, and great things have been achieved along that line. But the work in hand in business traffic is not tangible performance. The realities of the business world are money-values; that is to say matters of make-believe which have the sanction of law and custom and are upheld by the police in case of need. The business man's care is to create needs to be satisfied at a price paid to himself. The engineer's care is to provide for these needs, so far as the business men in the background find their advantage in allowing it. But law and custom have little to say to the engineer, except to keep his hands off the work when the interests of business call for a temperate scarcity.

So, by force of circumstances the captain of industry came in the course of time and growth to be occupied wholly with the financial end of those industrial ventures of which he still continued to be the captain. The spirit of enterprise in him took a turn of sobriety. He became patient and attentive to details, with an eye single to his own greater net gain in terms of price. His conduct came to be framed more and more on lines of an alert patience, moderation, assurance, and conservatism; that is to say, his conduct would have to fall into these lines if he was to continue as a Captain under the changing circumstances of the time. Changing circumstances called for a new line of strategy in those who would survive as Captains and come into the commanding positions in the business community, and so into control of the industrial system. It should perhaps rather be said that the force of changing circumstances worked a change in the character of the Captains by eliminating the Captains of the earlier type from the more responsible position and favoring the substitution of persons endowed with other gifts and trained to other ideals and other standards of conduct; in short, men more nearly on the order of safe and sane business, such as have continued to be well at home in responsible affairs since then.

Under the changing circumstances the captains of industry of the earlier type fell to second rank, became lieutenants, who presently more and more lost standing, as being irresponsible, fanciful project-makers, footless adventurers, fit only to work out innovations that were of doubtful expediency in a business way, creators of technological disturbances that led to obsolescence of equipment and therefore to shrinkage of assets. Such men are persons whom it is not for the safe and sane Captains of the newer type to countenance; but who should be handled with circumspection and made the most of, as project-makers whose restless initiative and immature versatility is counted on to bring about all sorts of unsettling and irritating changes in the conditions of industry; but who may also, now and again, bring in something that will give some patiently alert business man a new advantage over his rivals in business, if he has the luck or the shrewdness to grasp it firmly and betimes.

Under the changed circumstances the spirit of venturesome enterprise is more than likely to foot up a hunting of trouble, and wisdom in business enterprise has more and more settled down to the widsom of "Watchful waiting."[5]

The changing circumstances by force of which the conduct of industrial business so gradually came under the hands of a saner generation of Captains, actuated more singly by a conservative estimate of the net gain for themselves, — these circumstances have already been recited in an earlier passage, in sketching the rise and derivation of the business corporation and the conditions which brought corporation finance into action as the ordinary means of controlling the output of industry and turning it to the advantage of absentee owners. So far as these determining circumstances admit of being enumerated in an itemised way they were such as follows: (a) the industrial arts, in the mechanical industries, grew gradually into a complex and ex-

[5] Doubtless this form of words, "watchful waiting," will have been employed in the first instance to describe the frame of mind of a toad who has reached years of discretion and has found his appointed place along some frequented run where many flies and spiders pass and repass on their way to complete that destiny to which it has pleased an all-seeing and merciful Providence to call them; but by an easy turn of speech it has also been found suitable to describe the safe and sane strategy of that mature order of captains of industry who are governed by sound business principles. There is a certain bland sufficiency spread across the face of such a toad so circumstanced, while his comely personal bulk gives assurance of a pyramidal stability of principles.

"And the sons of Mary smile and are blessed —
    they know the angels are on their side,
They know in them is the Grace confessed,
    and for them are the Mercies multiplied.
They sit at the Feet, and they hear the Word —
    they know how truly the Promise runs.
They have cast their burden upon the Lord,
    and — the Lord, He lays it on Martha's sons."
                    — Rudyard Kipling

tensive technology which called for a continually more exhaustive and more exact knowledge of material facts, such as to give rise to engineers, technicians, industrial experts; (b) the scale on which industrial processes were carried out grew greater in the leading industries, so as to require the men in charge to give their undivided attention to the technical conduct, the tangible performance of the work in hand; (c) the business concerns in which was vested the ownership and control of the industrial equipment and its working also grew larger, carried a larger volume of transactions, took on more of an impersonally financial character, and eventually passed over into the wholly impersonal form of the corporation or joint-stock company, with limited liability; (d) the continued advance of the industrial arts, in range, scope, and efficiency, increased the ordinary productive capacity of the leading industries to such a degree that there was continually less and less question of their being able to supply the market and continually more and more danger that the output would exceed what the market could carry off at prices that would yield a reasonable profit — that is to say the largest obtainable profit; (e) loosely speaking, production had overtaken the market; (f) eventually corporation finance came into action and shifted the point of businesslike initiative and discretion from the works and their management, and even from the running volume of transactions carried by the business office of the concern, to the negotiation and maintenance of a running volume of credit; (g) the capitalisation of credit with fixed charges, as involved in the corporate organisation, precluded shrinkage, recession, or retrenchment of assets or earnings, and so ordinarily precluded a lowering of prices or an undue increase of output, — undue

for purposes of the net gain. Business enterprise, therefore, ceased progressively to be compatible with free-swung industrial enterprise, and a new order of businesslike management went progessively into action, and shuffled a new type of persons into the positions of responsibility; men with an eye more single to the main chance at the cost of any whom it may concern.

Among these circumstances that so made for a new order in industrial business the one which is, presumably, the decisive one beyond the rest is the growing productive capacity of industry wherever and so far as the later advances in industrial process are allowed to go into effect. By about the middle of the nineteenth century it can be said without affectation that the leading industries were beginning to be inordinately productive, as rated in terms of what the traffic would bear; that is to say as counted in terms of net gain. Free-swung production, approaching the full productive capacity of the equipment and available man-power, was no longer to be tolerated in ordinary times. It became ever more imperative to observe a duly graduated moderation, and to govern the volume of output, not by the productive capacity of the plant or the working capacity of the workmen, nor by the consumptive needs of the consumers, but by what the traffic would bear; which was then habitually and increasingly coming to mean a modicum of unemployment both of the plant and the available man-power. It was coming to be true, increasingly, that the ordinary equipment of industry and the available complement of workmen were not wanted for daily use, but only for special occasions and during seasons of exceptionally brisk trade. Unemployment, in other words sabotage, to use a word of later date, was becoming an everyday care of the business management in the mechanical industries, and was already on the way to become, what it is today, the most engrossing care that habitually engages the vigilance of the business executive. And sabotage can best be taken care of in the large; so that the corporations, and particularly the larger corporations, would be in a particularly fortunate position to administer the routine of salutary sabotage. And when the Captain of Industry then made the passage from industrial adventurer to corporation financier it became the ordinary care of his office as Captain to keep a restraining hand on employment and output, and so administer a salutary running margin of sabotage on production, at the cost of the underlying population.[6]

But the account is not complete with a description of what the Captain of industry has done toward the standardisation of business methods and the stabilisation of industrial enterprise, and of what the new order of business-as-usual has done toward the standardisation of the Captain and eventually towards his neutralisation and abeyance. As has already been remarked, he was one of the major institutions of the nineteenth century, and as such he has left his mark on the culture of that time and after, in other bearings as well as in the standards of business enterprise. As has also been remarked above, the Captain of Industry and his work and interests presently became the focus of attention and deference. The Landed Interest, the political buccaneers, and the priesthood, yielded him the first place in affairs and in the

councils of the nation, civil and political. With the forward movement from that state of things in which business was conceived to be the servant of industry to that more mature order of things under which industry became the servant of business, and then presently industrial business of the simpler sort became the servant of the big business which lives and moves on the higher level of finance at large, — as this progression took effect and reshaped the Captain to its uses, the growth of popular sentiment kept pace with the march of facts, so that the popular ideal came to be the prehensile business man rather than the creative driver of industry; the sedentary man of means, the Captain of Solvency. And all the while the illusions of nationalism allowed the underlying population to believe that the common good was bound up with the business advantage of these captains of solvency, into whose service the national establishment was gradually drawn, more and more unreservedly, until it has become an axiomatic rule that all the powers of government and diplomacy must work together for the benefit of the business interests of the larger sort. Not that the constituted authorities have no other cares, but these other cares are, after all, in all the civilised nations, in the nature of secondary considerations, matters to be taken care of when and so far as the paramount exigencies of business will allow.

In all this there is, of course, nothing radically new, in principle. In principle it all comes to much the same thing as the older plan which this era of business, big and little, has displaced. So long as nationalism has held sway, the care and affectionate pride of the underlying population has, in effect, ever centered on the due keep of the nation's kept classes. It is only that by force of circum-

---

[6] As someone with a taste for slang and aphorism has said it, "In the beginning the Captain of Industry set out to do something, and in the end he sat down to do somebody."

stances the captain of industry, or in more accurate words the captain of solvency, has in recent times come to be the effectual spokesman and type-form of the kept classes as well as the keeper and dispenser of their keep; very much as the War Lord of the barbarian raids, or the Baron of the Middle Ages, or the Prince of the era of state-making, or the Priesthood early and late in Christendom, have all and several, each in their time, place and degree, stood out as the spokesman and exemplar of the kept classes, and served as the legitimate channel by which the community's surplus product has been drained off and consumed, to the greater spiritual comfort of all parties concerned.

It is only that the superstitions of absentee ownership and business principles have come into the first place among those "Superstitions of the Herd" which go to make up the spirit of national integrity. The moral excellence and public utility of the kept classes that now march under the banners of absentee ownership and business enterprise are no more to be doubted by the loyal citizens of the Christian nations today than the similar excellence and utility of the princely establishment and the priestly ministrations which have drained the resources of the underlying population in an earlier and ruder age. And the princes of solvency and free income no more doubt their own excellence and utility than the princes of the divine grace or the prelates of the divine visitations have done in their time. It is only a shifting of the primacy among the civilised institutions, with the effect that the princes and the priests of the Grace and the Mercy now habitually creep in under the now impervious cloak of the prince and priest of business; very much as the business adventurer of an earlier day crept in

under the sheltering cloak of the prince and the priest of the Grace and the Mercy, on whom the superstitions that were dominant in that time then bestowed the usufruct of the underlying population. For in the nineteenth century the captain of business became, in the popular apprehension, a prince after the order of Melchizedech, holding the primacy in secular and spiritual concerns.

Men are moved by many impulses and driven by many instinctive dispositions. Among these abiding dispositions are a strong bent to admire and defer to persons of achievement and distinction, as well as a workmanlike disposition to find merit in any work that serves the common good. The distinction which is admired and deferred to may often be nothing more to the point than a conventional investiture of rank attained by the routine of descent, as, e.g., a king, or by the routine of seniority, as, e.g., a prelate. There is commonly no personal quality which a bystander can distinguish in these personages. The case of the Mikado in the times of the Shogunate is perhaps extreme, but it can by no means be said to be untrue or unfair as an illustrative instance of how the predilection for deference will find merit even in a personage who, for all that is known of him, has no personal attributes, good, bad, or indifferent. The kings and prelates of Christendom are only less perfect instances of the same. It is in these cases a matter of distinction, of course, with no hint of achievement, except such achievement as a loyal deference is bound to impute.[7]

7 As a blameless instance of this human avidity for deference and exaltation of personages, a certain Square on Manhattan Island has lately been renamed in honor of a certain military personage who was once, in an emergency, appointed to high rank and responsibility because there was nothing better available under the

It is usual, indeed it seems inevitable, in all such instances of the conventional exaltation of nothing-in-particular, that there is also imputed to the person who so becomes a personage something in the way of service to the common good. Men like to believe that the personages whom they so admire by force of conventional routine are also of some use, as well as of great distinction, — that they even somehow contribute, or at least conduce, to the material well-being at large. Which is presumably to be set down as one of the wonders wrought by the instinct of workmanship, which will not let men be content without some colorable serviceability in the personages which they so create out of nothing-in-particular.

But where there is also achievement, great deeds according to that fashion of exploits that has the vogue for the time being, this will of itself create distinction and erect a personage. Such is the derivation of the captain of industry in the nineteenth century. Men had learned, at some cost, that their exalted personages created *ad hoc* by incantation were of something less than no use to the common good, that at the best and cheapest they were something in the nature of a blameless bill of expense. The civilised nations had turned democratic, so much of them as had a fairly colorable claim to be called civilised; and so they had been left without their indispensable complement of personages to whom to defer and to whom to impute merit. In so far as the ground had been cleared of institutional holdovers from pre-democratic times, there remained but one workable ground of distinction on which a practicable line

of personages at large could be erected, such as would meet the ever-insistent need of some intoxicating make-believe of the kind. Democratically speaking, distinction at large could be achieved only in the matter of ownership, but when ownership was carried well out along the way of absentee ownership it was found to do very nicely as a base on which to erect a colorable personage, sufficient to carry a decently full charge of imputed merit.[8] It results that under the aegis of democracy one's betters must be better in point of property qualifications, from which the civic virtues flow by ready force of imputation.

So the captain of industry came into the place of first consequence and took up the responsibilities of exemplar, philosopher and friend at large to civilised mankind; and no man shall say that he has not done as well as might be expected. Neither has he fallen short in respect of a becoming gravity through it all. The larger the proportion of the community's wealth and income which he has taken over, the larger the deference and imputation of merit imputed to him, and the larger and graver that affable condescension and stately benevolence that habitually adorn the character of the large captains of solvency. There is no branch or department of the humanities in which the substantial absentee owner is not competent to act as guide, philoso-

---

routine of seniority, and of whose deeds and attainments the most laudatory encomium has found nothing substantially better to say than that it might have been worse. And it is by no means an isolated case.

[8] Exception may be taken to all this, to the effect that the requisite personages can always be found in the shape of gentlemen at large — "country gentlemen" or "Southern Gentlemen," or what not — and "Best Families" who sit secure on a prescriptive gentility of birth and breeding. But in this bearing and seen in impersonal perspective, Gentlemen and Best Families are best to be defined as "absentee ownership in the consumptive phase," just as the captain of industry may likewise be spoken of impersonally as absentee ownership in the acquisitive phase; which brings the case back to the point of departure.

pher and friend, whether in his own conceit or in the estimation of his underlying population, — in art and literature, in church and state, in science and education, in law and morals, — and the underlying population is well content. And nowhere does the pecuniary personage stand higher or more secure as the standard container of the civic virtues than in democratic America; as should be the case, of course, since America is the most democratic of them all. And nowhere else does the captain of big business rule the affairs of the nation, civil and political, and control the conditions of life so unreservedly as in democratic America; as should also be the case, inasmuch as the acquisition of absentee ownership is, after all, in the popular apprehension, the most meritorious and the most necessary work to be done in this country.

Finley Peter Dunne:

THE CARNEGIE LIBRARIES

"HAS Andhrew Carnaygie given ye a libry yet?" asked Mr. Dooley.

"Not that I know iv," said Mr. Hennessy.

"He will," said Mr. Dooley. "Ye'll not escape him. Befure he dies he hopes to crowd a libry on ivry man, woman, an' child in th' counthry. He's given thim to cities, towns, villages, an' whistlin' stations. They're tearin' down gas-houses an' poorhouses to put up libries. Befure another year, ivry house in Pittsburg that ain't a blast-furnace will be a Carnaygie libry. In some places all th' buildin's is libries. If ye write him f'r an autygraft he sinds ye a libry. No beggar is iver turned impty-handed fr'm th' dure. Th' pan-handler knocks an' asts f'r a glass iv milk an' a roll. 'No, sir,' says Andhrew Carnaygie. 'I will not pauperize this onworthy man. Nawthin' is worse f'r a beggar-man thin to make a pauper iv him. Yet it shall not be said iv me that I give nawthin' to th' poor. Saunders, give him a libry, an' if he still insists on a roll tell him to roll th' libry. F'r I'm humorous as well as wise,' he says."

"Does he give th' books that go with it?" asked Mr. Hennessy.

"Books?" said Mr. Dooley. "What ar-re ye talkin' about? D'ye know what a libry is? I suppose ye think it's a place where a man can go, haul down wan iv his fav'rite authors fr'm th' shelf, an' take a nap in it. That's not a Carnaygie libry. A Carnaygie libry is a large, brown-stone, impenethrible buildin' with th' name iv th' maker blown on th' dure. Libry, fr'm th' Greek wurruds, libus, a book, an' ary, sildom, — sildom a book. A Carnaygie libry is archytechoor, not lithrachoor. Lithrachoor will be riprisinted. Th' most cillybrated dead authors will be honored be havin' their names painted on th' wall in distinguished comp'ny, as thus: Andhrew Carnaygie, Shakespeare; Andhrew Carnaygie, Byron; Andhrew Carnaygie, Bobby Burns; Andhrew Carnaygie, an' so on. Ivry author is guaranteed a place next to pure readin' matther like a bakin'-powdher advertisemint, so that whin a man comes along that niver heerd iv Shakespeare he'll know he was somebody, because there he is on th' wall. That's th' dead authors. Th' live authors will stand outside an' wish they were dead.

"He's havin' gr-reat spoort with it. I r-read his speech th' other day, whin he laid th' corner-stone iv th' libry at Pianola, Ioway. Th' entire popylation iv this lithry cinter gathered to see an' hear him. There was th' postmaster an' his wife, th' blacksmith an' his fam'ly, the station agent, mine host iv th' Farmers' Exchange, an' some sthray live stock. 'Ladies an' gintlemen,' says he. 'Modesty compels me to say nawthin' on this occasion, but I am not to be bulldozed,' he says. 'I can't tell ye how much pleasure I take in disthributin' monymints to th' humble name around which has gathered so manny hon'rable associations with me-silf. I have been a very busy little man all me life, but I like hard wurruk, an' givin' away me money is th' hardest wurruk I iver did. It fairly makes me teeth ache to part with it. But there's wan consolation. I cheer mesilf with th' thought that no matther how much money I give it don't do anny particular person anny good. Th' worst thing ye can do f'r anny man is to do him good. I pass by th' organ-grinder on th' corner with a savage glare. I bate th' monkey on th' head whin he comes up smilin' to me window, an' hurl him down on his impecyoonyous owner. None iv me money goes into th' little tin cup. I cud kick a hospital, an' I lave Wall Sthreet to look afther th' widow an' th' orphan. Th' submerged tenth, thim that can't get hold iv a good chunk iv th' goods, I wud cut off fr'm th' rest iv th' wurruld an' pre-vint fr'm bearin' th' haughty name iv papa or th' still lovelier name iv ma. So far I've got on'y half me wish in this matther.

" 'I don't want poverty an' crime to go on. I intind to stop it. But how? It's been holdin' its own f'r cinchries. Some iv th' gr-reatest iv former minds has un-dertook to prevint it an' has failed. They didn't know how. Modesty wud prevint me agin fr'm sayin' that I know how, but that's nayether here nor there. I do. Th' way to abolish poverty an' bust crime is to put a brown-stone buildin' in ivry town in th' counthry with me name over it. That's th' way. I suppose th' raison it wasn't thried befure was that no man iver had such a name. 'Tis thrue me efforts is not apprecyated ivrywhere. I offer a city a libry, an' oftentimes it replies an'

asks me f'r something to pay off th' school debt. I rayceive degraded pettyshuns fr'm so-called proud methropolises f'r a gas-house in place iv a libry. I pass thim by with scorn. All I ask iv a city in ray-turn f'r a fifty-thousan'-dollar libry is that it shall raise wan millyon dollars to main-tain th' buildin' an' keep me name shiny, an' if it won't do that much f'r lithra-choor, th' divvle take it, it's onworthy iv th' name iv an American city. What ivry community needs is taxes an' lithrachoor. I give thim both. Three cheers f'r a libry an' a bonded debt! Lithrachoor, taxation, an' Andhrew Carnaygie, wan an' insipra-ble, now an' foriver! They'se nawthin' so good as a good book. It's betther thin food; it's betther thin money. I have made money an' books, an' I like me books betther thin me money. Others don't, but I do. With these few wurruds I will con-clude. Modesty wud prevint me fr'm sayin' more, but I have to catch a thrain, an' cannot go on. I stake ye to this libry, which ye will have as soon as ye raise th' money to keep it goin'. Stock it with useful readin', an' some day ye're otherwise pauper an' criminal childher will come to know me name whin I am gone an' there's no wan left to tell it thim.'

"Whin th' historyan comes to write th' histhry iv th' West he'll say: 'Pianola, Ioway, was a prosperous town till th' failure iv th' corn crop in nineteen hun-dherd an' wan, an' th' Carnaygie libry in nineteen hundherd an' two. Th' gov-ermint ast f'r thirty dollars to pave Main Sthreet with wooden blocks, but th' gr-reat philanthropist was firm, an' the libry was sawed off on th' town. Th' public schools, th' wurruk-house, th' wather wurruks, an' th' other penal insti-choochions was at wanst closed, an' th' people begun to wurruk to support th' libry. In five years th' popylation had deserted th' town to escape taxation, an' now, as Mr. Carnaygie promised, poverty an' crime has been abolished in th' place, th' janitor iv th' buildin' bein' honest an' well paid.'

"Isn't it good f'r lithrachoor, says ye? Sure, I think not, Hinnissy. Libries niver encouraged lithrachoor anny more thin tombstones encourage livin'. No wan iver wrote annythin' because he was tol' that a hundherd years fr'm now his books might be taken down fr'm a shelf in a granite sepulcher an' some wan wud write 'Good' or 'This man is crazy' in th' margin. What lithrachoor needs is fillin' food. If Andhrew wud put a kitchen in th' libries an' build some bunks or even swing a few hammocks where livin' authors cud crawl in at night an' sleep while waitin' f'r this enlightened nation to wake up an' discover th' Shakespeares now on th' turf, he wud be givin' a rale boost to lithrachoor. With th' smoke curlin' fr'm th' chimbley, an' hundherds iv potes settin' aroun' a table loaded down with pancakes an' talkin' pothry an' prize-fightin', with hundherds iv other potes, stacked up nately in th' sleepin'-rooms an' snorin' in wan gran' chorus, with their wives holdin' down good-payin' jobs as libraryans or cooks, an' their happy little childher playin' through th' marble corridors, Andhrew Carnaygie wud not have lived in vain. Maybe that's th' on'y way he knows how to live. I don't believe in libries. They pauperize lithrachoor. I'm f'r helpin' th' boys that's now on th' job. I know a pote in Halsted Sthreet that wanst wrote a pome beginnin', 'All th' wealth iv Ind,' that he sold to a magazine f'r two dollars, payable on publycation. Lithrachoor don't need advancin'. What it needs is advances f'r th' lithrachoors. Ye can't shake down posterity f'r th' price.

"All th' same, I like Andhrew Carnaygie. Him an' me ar-re agreed on that point. I like him because he ain't shamed to give publicly. Ye don't find him puttin' on false whiskers an' turnin' up his coat-collar whin he goes out to be benivolent. No, sir. Ivry time he dhrops a dollar it makes a noise like a waither fallin' down-stairs with a tray iv dishes. He's givin' th' way we'd all like to give. I niver put annythin' in th' poor-box, but I wud if Father Kelly wud rig up like wan iv thim slot-machines, so that whin I stuck in a nickel me name wud appear over th' altar in red letthers. But whin I put a dollar in th' plate I get back about two yards an' hurl it so hard that th' good man turns around to see who done it. Do good be stealth, says I, but see that th' burglar-alarm is set. Anny benivolent money I hand out I want to talk about me. Him that giveth to th' poor, they say, lindeth to th' Lord; but in these days we look f'r quick returns on our invistmints. I like Andhrew Carnaygie, an', as he says, he puts his whole soul into th' wurruk."

"What's he mane be that?" asked Mr. Hennessy.

"He manes," said Mr. Dooley, "that he's gin'rous. Ivry time he gives a libry he gives himsilf away in a speech."

Suggestions for Additional Reading

A good introduction to the period and the problem with which this volume is concerned is the final chapter, "Traditions of Democracy," in Arthur M. Schlesinger, Jr., *The Age of Jackson* (Boston, 1945). There is a brilliant characterization of the Gilded Age in chapter 25 of Charles and Mary Beard, *The Rise of American Civilization* (New York, 1930). All of the relevant chapters in this book are excellent for general background.

The most recent and comprehensive account of the intellectual history of the period is Merle Curti, *The Growth of American Thought* (New York and London, 1943). The books by Parrington and Gabriel from which sections are reprinted above contain much valuable material in addition to those sections. Lewis Mumford in *The Brown Decades* (New York, 1931) attempts to characterize the period in terms of its arts and architecture; and Granville Hicks has a parallel discussion of literature in *The Great Tradition* (New York, 1933).

Thomas C. Cochran and William Miller in *The Age of Enterprise* (New York, 1942) give a good general description of the development of modern industrialism in America. Andrew Carnegie's own version of this story is to be found in *Triumphant Democracy or Fifty Years' March of the Republic* (New York, 1886). Matthew Josephson's *The Robber Barons* (New York, 1934) is a lively account of the exploits of the great captains of industry.

For the relation of capitalism to religion consult Max Weber, *The Protestant Ethic and the Spirit of Capitalism,* translated by Talcott Parsons (New York, 1930), and R. H. Tawney, *Religion and the Rise of Capitalism* (New York, 1926). For a briefer treatment of this subject see Erich Fromm, *Escape from Freedom* (New York, 1941), chapters 3, 4.

The most comprehensive survey of the influence of the theory of evolution as it was applied by Herbert Spencer and others to social problems, is Richard Hofstadter, *Social Darwinism in American Thought — 1860–1915* (Philadelphia, 1944). Briefer accounts will be found in chapter 22 of Curti, "Evolutionary Thought in a Utilitarian Society," and chapter 6 of Cochran and Miller, "A Philosophy for Industrial Enterprise."

The more important of the "success books" are described by Gabriel in the chapter on the gospel of wealth included in this volume. Russell H. Conwell's lecture, "Acres of Diamonds," a piece as famous as "A Message to Garcia," is reprinted in *Modern Eloquence*, T. B. Reed, ed. (Philadelphia, 1900–03, 15 vols.), IV, 307–338. Literature of this type is a hardy perennial. Two of the most conspicuous recent examples are: Bruce Barton, *The Man Nobody Knows: A Discovery of Jesus* (Indianapolis, 1925), and the book everybody knows, Dale Carnegie, *How to Win Friends and Influence People* (New York, 1936).

One of the first and most important discussions of the impact of industrial capitalism upon a democratic social order is Henry George's *Progress and Poverty* (San Francisco, 1879). William Demarest Lloyd's *Wealth against Commonwealth* (New York, 1894) is a powerful indictment of monopolies, in particular the Standard Oil trust, which anticipated the writings of the "Muckrakers"; Thorstein Veblen's *The Theory of the Leisure Class* (New York, 1899) is a mordantly satirical analysis of the way in which the pecuniary standards dominate in our society; W. J. Ghent's *Our Benevolent Feudalism* (New York, 1902) expands and develops the theme of the article printed in this volume; Frederick Townsend Martin's *The Passing of the Idle Rich* (New York, 1911) gives a sensational account of the extravagancies and frivolities of the newly rich.

A good account of the reaction to these attacks may be found in chapter 25 of Curti's book, "The Conservative Defense," and in chapters 18 and 19 of Gabriel, "The Gospel of Wealth and American Constitutional Law" and "William Graham Sumner: Critic of Romantic Democracy." Andrew Carnegie, *The Empire of Business* (New York, 1902), gives a more elaborate statement of his views. A contemporary defense in terms closely similar to those used by Carnegie is Carl Snyder, *Capitalism the Creator* (New York, 1940).

Biographies and novels are among the best sources for an understanding of this problem. Henry Adams's autobiography, *The Education of Henry Adams* (Boston, 1918; first printed privately in 1906), is the most profound book dealing with the period. Some other useful biographical works are: Andrew Carnegie, *Autobiography* (Boston and New York, 1920); John T. Flynn's biography of Rockefeller, *God's Gold* (New York, 1932); Frederick Lewis Allen, *The Great Pierpont Morgan* (New York, 1949); Robert M. La Follette, *Autobiography* (Madison, 1913); Joseph Dorfman, *Thorstein Veblen and His America* (New York, 1934); Lincoln Steffens, *Autobiography* (New York, 1931); Elmer Ellis, *Mr. Dooley's America: A Life of Finley Peter Dunne* (New York, 1941).

Some of the more important novels dealing with one aspect or another of the gospel of wealth are: Mark Twain and Charles Dudley Warner, *The Gilded Age* (1873); Henry Adams, *Democracy* (1880); William Dean Howells, *The Rise of Silas Lapham* (1885); Edward Bellamy, *Looking Backward, 2000–1887* (1888); Frank Norris, *The Octopus* (1901) and *The Pit* (1903); Upton Sinclair, *The Jungle* (1906); Theodore Dreiser, *The Financier* (1912) and *The Titan* (1914); Sinclair Lewis, *Babbitt* (1922).

The most recent and adequate bibliographies dealing with this problem are those in Curti's *Growth of American Thought*.

ASSIGNED READIN   RULES